NINETEENTH-CENTURY RUSSIA:
OPPOSITION TO AUTOCRACY

Nineteenth-Century Russia: Opposition to Autocracy

DEREK OFFORD

LONGMAN

Pearson Education Limited,
Edinburgh Gate,
Harlow,
Essex CM20 2JE,
United Kingdom
and Associated Companies throughout the world.

*Published in the United States of America
by Pearson Education Inc, New York*

© Pearson Education Limited 1999

First published 1999

ISBN 0 582 35767 5

Visit our world wide web site at http://www.awl-he.com

British Library Cataloguing-in-Publication Data
A catalogue record for this book is available from the British Library

Library of Congress Cataloging-in-Publication Data
A catalogue record for this book is available from the Library of Congress

Set by 7 in 10/12 Sabon
Printed in Malaysia (PP)

CONTENTS

An introduction to the series   vii
Note on referencing system   viii
Note on dates, transliteration and use of Russian terms   ix
Foreword   xi
Map: Nineteenth-century Russia   xiii

PART ONE: THE HISTORICAL SETTING   **1**

1. THE POLITICAL AND SOCIAL STRUCTURE   1
   Autocracy   1
   Nobility and service   2
   Serfdom and social backwardness   3

2. CULTURAL AND INTELLECTUAL LIFE   7
   Westernization   7
   The intelligentsia   9

PART TWO: PHASES OF OPPOSITION   **12**

3. THE AGE OF ALEXANDER I (1801–25)   12
   The 'fine beginning of Alexander's days'   12
   The Decembrist Revolt   13

4. THE AGE OF NICHOLAS I (1825–55)   20
   Russian culture in the age of Nicholas   20
   Chaadaev's 'Philosophical Letter'   23
   Slavophilism   25
   Liberal Westernizers   29
   Belinsky   33
   Herzen   37
   The Petrashevtsy   41

5. INTELLECTUAL REVOLT (1855–c. 1868)   44
    The effects and aftermath of the Crimean War   44
    Conservative nationalist thought in the 1850s and 1860s   48
    Russian liberalism after the Crimean War   50
    Radical thought: Chernyshevsky   55
    Radical thought: Dobroliubov, Pisarev and the arts   59
    Seditious literature and revolutionary groups in the 1860s   62

6. THE REVOLUTIONARY MOVEMENT IN THE 1870s   66
    Radical literature and thought, 1868–73   66
    Lavrov   68
    Bakunin   70
    Tkachov   72
    The 'going to the people'   75
    Land and Liberty   78
    The People's Will, 1879–81   81

7. OPPOSITION AFTER 1881   85
    Tolstoy   85
    Plekhanov and the 'Emancipation of Labour' Group   88
    Revolutionary groups in the 1880s   92
    Political movements in the 1890s   97

    PART THREE: ASSESSMENT   102

    PART FOUR: DOCUMENTS   106

    Bibliography   126
    Index   136

AN INTRODUCTION TO THE SERIES

Such is the pace of historical enquiry in the modern world that there is an ever-widening gap between the specialist article or monograph, incorporating the results of current research, and general surveys, which inevitably become out of date. *Seminar Studies in History* are designed to bridge this gap. The series was founded by Patrick Richardson in 1966 and his aim was to cover major themes in British, European and World history. Between 1980 and 1996 Roger Lockyer continued his work, before handing the editorship over to Clive Emsley and Gordon Martel. Clive Emsley is Professor of History at the Open University, while Gordon Martel is Professor of International History at the University of Northern British Columbia, Canada and Senior Research Fellow at De Montfort University.

All the books are written by experts in their field who are not only familiar with the latest research but have often contributed to it. They are frequently revised, in order to take account of new information and interpretations. They provide a selection of documents to illustrate major themes and provoke discussion, and also a guide to further reading. The aim of *Seminar Studies* is to clarify complex issues without over-simplifying them, and to stimulate readers into deepening their knowledge and understanding of major themes and topics.

NOTE ON REFERENCING SYSTEM

Readers should note that numbers in square brackets [5] refer them to the corresponding entry in the Bibliography at the end of the book (specific page numbers are given in italics). A number in square brackets preceded by *Doc.* [*Doc.* 5] refers readers to the corresponding item in the Documents section which follows the main text.

NOTE ON DATES, TRANSLITERATION AND USE OF RUSSIAN TERMS

DATES

Dates given in the text are as a rule in the Old Style (OS) – that is, according to the Julian calendar which was used in nineteenth-century Russia. In the nineteenth century the Julian calendar was twelve days behind the Gregorian calendar that was used then, as now, in Western Europe. The Bolsheviks replaced the Julian calendar with the Gregorian calendar in February 1918. Dates of events taking place outside Russia are given in the New Style, indicated by the abbreviation NS.

TRANSLITERATION

Russian names and terms are transliterated from the Cyrillic in this book, broadly speaking, according to the Library of Congress system. However, the ending -sky, which is familiar to English readers, is retained in Russian surnames (e.g. Dostoevsky, instead of the more correct form Dostoevskii). The familiar form Tolstoy is preferred to Tolstoi. The Russian letter ë is rendered by io (e.g. Ogariov) or, after hushing consonants, by o (e.g. Tkachov), thus giving a better indication of the sound represented by the letter than the rendering e. Russian soft signs are not transliterated in names of people or places but are rendered by an apostrophe in Anglicized versions of other Russian words (e.g. glasnost'). The name Gertsen is rendered in the commonly accepted Germanized form Herzen.

USE OF RUSSIAN TERMS

Titles of journals are given in English translation, but the transliterated Russian form of the title is also given in each instance when the

journal is mentioned for the first time in the text, e.g. *The Contemporary*
(*Sovremennik*). Titles of all other works in Russian or any other language are given only in English. The meaning of Russian terms is
explained when the term is first used in the text. A number of Russian
words ending in the suffix *-ets* (plural *-tsy*) are retained: these words
indicate a person or persons of a particular origin (e.g. *raznochinets*,
member of a social stratum beneath the gentry) or a person or persons
associated with a particular individual (e.g. Nechaevtsy, people associated with Nechaev).

FOREWORD

The purpose of this work is to provide a brief survey of the development of opposition to the autocratic state in nineteenth-century Russia. The book identifies the most prominent landmarks in the history of that opposition, such as the Decembrist Revolt of 1825, the 'going to the people' of 1874 and the assassination of Alexander II in 1881; it examines the major thinkers and groups of thinkers who challenged the legitimacy of the regime; and it describes the main organizations which, particularly in the second half of the century, sought in one way or another to undermine it. It should be stressed, though, that it is with opposition as articulated and organized by the educated class that the book is concerned. It does not chronicle the history of less conscious opposition to the regime by the peasantry (among whom there were sporadic outbreaks of violence) or the factory workers (among whom there began to develop in the second half of the century a labour movement that was to a considerable extent independent of the intelligentsia).

Coverage of such a broad subject as opposition to autocracy in nineteenth-century Russia within the framework of a monograph of this size is necessarily somewhat superficial. It is hoped though that some of the major themes, preoccupations and dilemmas of Russian thinkers will emerge, for example: the relationship of Russia to the West; the related question of the value of the heritage of the Westernizing ruler Peter the Great; the relationship between the educated class and the inarticulate masses; the nature of those masses; the extent to which individuals and whole peoples have freedom to shape their destinies; and the relationship between individuals and the collectivity to which they belong. Furthermore the bibliography should lead the student to works that explore each important aspect of the subject in greater depth.

My thanks are due to Clive Emsley, the series editor, and Hilary Shaw, the commissioning editor, for their encouragement of the project and for their useful suggestions, and to Sally Steen for help in preparation of parts of the typescript. I am also grateful to my colleagues Michael Basker and Richard Buxton for advice on matters of detail. Responsibility for all errors and flaws of interpretation and presentation is of course mine alone.

Map xiii

Nineteenth-century Russia

PART ONE: THE HISTORICAL SETTING

1 THE POLITICAL AND SOCIAL STRUCTURE

AUTOCRACY

In order to understand the rich cultural and intellectual life that flowered in nineteenth-century Russia and the forms taken by the political opposition to which that life gave rise, we need briefly to consider the country's political and social structure.

Throughout the nineteenth century, and indeed down to the February Revolution of 1917, Russia continued to be governed by an autocrat. That is to say, supreme legislative, executive and judicial power rested in the hands of a monarch who was the sole source of law in the state and was accountable to no-one for the way in which he exercised his authority. (As Leonard Schapiro has pointed out, the Russian word for 'state', *gosudarstvo*, derived from the word for 'sovereign' (*gosudar'*), suggests this association of the individual ruler with the polity as a whole [39 *p. 78*].) Nineteenth-century Russia, then, did not have citizens; rather the Russian tsar (or emperor as he was also known after 1722, when Peter I adopted the title following his victory in the Great Northern War with Sweden) had subjects who owed him unconditional obedience and of whom he could dispose as he pleased.

The institution of autocracy in Russia had developed over a long period following the throwing-off of the Tatar yoke under which Russia laboured from *c.* 1240 to *c.* 1480 and the emergence of the grand princes of Moscow as the claimants to power in the post-Tatar state. It is reasonable to argue that the harshness of the institution of autocracy in Russia was to a considerable extent the product of that long domination by the infidel nomads and the difficulty of the conditions in which the Muscovite state developed. The process of constructing a centralized autocratic state was completed in the sixteenth century by Ivan IV (Ivan the Terrible, who ruled from 1533 to 1584). The power of the autocrat and the severity with which it was wielded were in no way lessened by Peter the Great (sole ruler from 1696 to 1725), despite his far-reaching attempt to Westernize Russia in the first quarter of the eighteenth century. Peter's reign is notable for the dragooning of subjects into state service of one sort or another; the brutal crushing of revolts and political opposition, real or imagined; the ruthless expenditure of human life on projects such as the fortification of the country and the construction of St Petersburg which Peter considered of paramount importance to his state; and the regimentation of the populace and the application of discipline of a military type to all areas of national life [32]. Throughout the eighteenth century forces that in the West counterbalanced the power of the state, such as an independent legal profession, advanced private education, a powerful Church, a broad reading public or a middle class, were relatively weak in Russia [61 *p.* 22]. Alexander I (ruled 1801–25) and Alexander II (ruled 1855–81), in the early years of their respective reigns, did give enlightened opinion of the time some hope that the autocrat himself would limit the sovereign's power. Meanwhile a developing political opposition – represented, for example, by the Decembrists of 1825, the radical thinkers of the 1850s and 1860s and the revolutionaries active from the 1860s on – hoped either to wring concessions from or altogether to destroy the autocracy. And yet no reform in nineteenth-century Russia eroded the authority of the autocrat nor was any major political concession wrung from the government. Moreover, throughout the century the autocrat had at his disposal a powerful military force, a large – though inefficient – bureaucracy, and further instruments of control, such as a large secret police force, an army of informers, and powers of censorship, which at certain periods – for example at the beginning of the reign of Nicholas I (ruled 1825–55) – were strengthened or deployed with increased vigour.

NOBILITY AND SERVICE

Autocracy depended on the support of the nobility. In Muscovite Russia the privileged position of the great noble clans had been bolstered by a complex system of precedence (*mestnichestvo*), introduced in the fifteenth century, of which the autocrat was obliged to take account when making high appointments or arranging ceremonial functions at court. However, already in the sixteenth century, particularly in the reign of Ivan IV, there emerged alongside those who were noble by virtue of their pedigree a new class (*dvorianstvo*) that had attained noble status by means of loyal service to the state in the person of the ruler. This class was rewarded with the allocation of land held as a fief (*pomest'e*) which remained the legal property of the tsar and which differed from the patrimonial estate (*votchina*) held in perpetuity by the old boyar clans [39 *pp. 92 ff.*]. Although *mestnichestvo* continued to flourish in the seventeenth century, it was finally abolished in 1682 and shortly afterwards Peter the Great took steps, as Ivan had done, to ensure that his nobility gave unstinting service to the state. His Entail Law of 1714, prohibiting the division of a nobleman's estate on his death and requiring that the estate be bequeathed in its entirety to only one of the nobleman's sons, left the remaining sons available for state service. His Table of Ranks, published in 1722, according to which fourteen ranks were created in each of the three areas in which service to the state could be given – the civil service, the army, and the navy (which Peter himself had created) – firmly established the relationship between service and rank [32 *pp. 188–93*; 34 i, *pp. 420–21*; 47 *pp. 155–7*].

Peter's successors came under pressure to relax the demands on the nobility. Thus in 1736, under the Empress Anna (ruled 1730–40), the period of compulsory state service was reduced to twenty-five years; in 1762 a manifesto issued by Peter III (ruled 1761–62) altogether abolished the requirement that nobles serve the state; and in 1785, in her 'Charter of the Nobility', Catherine II (ruled 1762–96) confirmed the exemption from service and other privileges of the nobility. That is not to say that all nobles in fact ceased to serve, although many in the late eighteenth century and the nineteenth century served only in a desultory way and for a short period. Nevertheless the abolition of the ancient obligation to serve did create an idle class, a minority of whom used their leisure and resources to cultivate themselves but many of whom lacked a sense of purpose. In the nineteenth century, if we are to judge by his portrayal in the imaginative literature of the age, the nobleman exempt from service was prone to an ennui nourished by Western fashions. At the same time in many noblemen a sense of obligation remained strong and this sense, no longer channelled by the state, began to find expression in an interest in ideas and ideals that were ultimately to prove destructive to the autocratic state [42].

SERFDOM AND SOCIAL BACKWARDNESS

The autocrat had a further means of rewarding service, apart from land and status, namely the award of serfs to tend the noble's estate, or estates, and to wait upon him and his family in his manor (*usad'ba*). The gradual development of serfdom in post-Tatar Muscovy is indicated in edicts of the fifteenth and sixteenth centuries (e.g. 1497, 1550, 1597) which place increasing restrictions on the movement of the peasant population. The existence of serfdom in its full-blown form is registered by the legal code, or *ulozhenie*, issued in 1649 under Alexis (ruled 1645–76), which confirmed the landowner's status as absolute and unconditional master of his peasants and tax-gatherer for the tsar [33]. Thus by the beginning of the nineteenth century the nobleman wielded on his own estate an absolute power comparable to that exercised by the tsar in Russia as a whole. He had full legal authority over his serfs and was able to sell them – breaking up families in the process – or give them away as gifts or in settlement of debts, inflict corporal punishment on them or have them sent into the armed forces or to penal labour in Siberia. An advertisement placed in a late eighteenth-century newspaper attests to the status of the serf as chattel:

> For sale: domestics and skilled craftsmen of good behaviour, viz. two tailors, a shoemaker, a watchmaker, a cook, a coachmaker, a wheelwright, an engraver, a gilder, and two coachmen, who may be inspected and their price ascertained . . . at the proprietor's own house, No. 51. Also for sale are three young racehorses, one colt and two geldings, and a pack of hounds, fifty in number, which will be a year old in January and February next. [quoted in 111 *p. 33*]

The serf tied to the estate of a nobleman had an onerous obligation towards his master. This obligation took the form of either *barshchina*, a labour-due similar to the Western *corvée*, or *obrok*, similar to the Western quit-rent, that is to say an obligation to deliver to the landowner some combination of money and payment in kind. Although the Emperor Paul (ruled 1796–1801) stated that a serf should be required to work for his master for no more than three days each week, in practice such laws could not rigorously be enforced since the judiciary was itself drawn from the landowning class. The labour due, *barshchina*, was generally considered the more onerous of the two obligations and landowners of liberal temper sometimes transferred their peasants to *obrok*. In the main, though, the prevalence of one type of obligation or another in a region was determined by the relationship between the local agricultural conditions and the interest of the landowning class: where the land was fertile, especially in the rich black-earth belt, *barshchina* tended to prevail, whilst in less fertile regions *obrok* was more widespread. It should be added that every male serf was obliged to pay a tax to the state, that is the poll-tax (*podushnaia podat'*), introduced by Peter the Great following the census begun in 1718 and first levied in 1724. He was also liable to military recruitment for a term of twenty-five years, if he was taken to serve in the army, or ten years if he was taken to serve in the navy where conditions were still harsher. Protest at this state of affairs, in the form of localized eruptions of violence, was a commonplace feature of Russian rural life. A more serious danger, of which government and nobles were ever conscious, was recurrence of elemental peasant revolt of the sort that had erupted with an almost fatal regularity in the sixteenth and seventeenth centuries. These revolts – led by Bolotnikov in 1606–7, Stenka Razin in 1671–72, Bulavin in 1707–9 and Pugachov in 1773–74 – emanated from the Russian heartland in the South East, in the regions of the Volga and the Don. They attracted large, unsettled, drifting sections of the population and serfs in those regions, unleashed a tide of savage destructive energy and, in the case of the revolts of Stenka Razin and Pugachov, were put down by the state only with great difficulty.

It is impossible to overstate the importance of the late survival in Russia of serfdom, an institution that in Western Europe is associated with medieval, feudal times and had begun to decline from the end of the thirteenth century. (In Eastern Europe the institution had persisted much longer, but even in the Austro-Hungarian Empire it had been abolished in the late eighteenth century.) Its persistence in Russia until 1861 had profound adverse moral and social consequences. For one thing serfdom was felt to degrade the serf-owning class itself. The existence of a servile mass dedicated to the task of providing for a privileged minority fostered indolence and dependency in many landowners. Some, like the notoriously cruel mother of the novelist Turgenev [62 *pp. 16–17*], were clearly brutalized by their absolute power over their serfs. In a minority – and it is from this minority that some of the most articulate opponents of autocracy were to come – the power they involuntarily wielded over fellow human beings induced a crushing sense of guilt. On a broader level the persistence of serfdom inhibited the spread of literacy, education and civic consciousness. Among the mass of the population an independent spirit could therefore find expression only more or less outside the jurisdiction of the state, among the Cossacks who settled at Russia's frontiers, in the sectarian communities that had sprung up following the schism (*raskol*) precipitated in the Russian Church in the second half of the seventeenth century by the reforms of Patriarch Nikon [34 i, *pp. 286–95*], and among the criminal elements of society idealized in the second half of the nineteenth century by revolutionary anarchists.

Most importantly, serfdom was associated with economic backwardness. By tying the bulk of the population to the land and preventing the movement of a free labour force, it acted as an impediment to the growth of towns and the development of industry and modern communications. Whereas the ratio of townsmen to villagers in 1840 was roughly one to two in Britain and one to five in France, in Russia it was one to over eleven [44 *pp. 142–3*]. The proportion of the population that could be classified as factory workers was relatively small and industry was often of the cottage variety. Construction of a railway line between St Petersburg and Moscow did not begin until 1842 [45 *p. 247*]. This retarded economic development may in turn be associated with the lack of a coherent middle class or bourgeoisie. Even late in the nineteenth century the elements that in the West comprised a middle class – business people, bureaucrats, professionals and intellectuals – tended in Russia to be disparate and to pursue different interests [45 *pp. 28–9*]. This social lacuna had a profound effect on political as well as economic development. It accounts for the relative weakness in nineteenth-century Russia of moderate, liberal political opinion. It may also explain the lack of sympathy shown by thinkers at both ends of the political spectrum for entrepreneurial activity, the lack of practicality in much of their thought – which tends towards the visionary rather than the concrete – and their disdain, even contempt, for prosperity and material gain.

2 CULTURAL AND INTELLECTUAL LIFE

WESTERNIZATION

Political and social backwardness in pre-revolutionary Russia cannot be divorced from the late arrival there of secular learning and culture. The domination of Russia by the Tatars for over two hundred years had the effect of cutting Russia off from the West at the time of the Renaissance and severely retarded the progress of intellectual and cultural life. In Kievan times (from the tenth to the twelfth centuries) the earliest Russian state had enjoyed contacts – commercial, cultural, religious and even dynastic – with many other peoples. In Muscovite times (from the fourteenth to the seventeenth centuries), on the other hand, the Russians did not participate in the remarkable geographical exploration, scientific discovery, flowering of commerce, architecture and painting, rediscovery of classical learning, and development of scholarship, secular literary traditions, theology and philosophy which were taking place in the West in those centuries. Admittedly a written literary tradition was kept alive in Russia during the dark age of the Tatar yoke by the monasteries, whose existence the Tatars tolerated. However, Russia had drawn its Christianity – in 988 according to the chronicles, during the rule of the Kievan Prince Vladimir – from Byzantium in the East rather than Rome in the West, and in 1054 the growing schism between the Western, Catholic branch of the Christian Church and its Eastern, Orthodox branch was formalized by a papal bull excommunicating the Eastern Church. The Russian Orthodox Church, which laid claim to leadership of the Christian world when Constantinople fell to the Muslim Turks in 1453, harboured deep suspicions of alien influences, set no store by the intellectual interests fostered by the Western Church, defended a pre-scientific, superstitious view of the world and opposed the dissemination in Russia of secular learning and art. Not until the reign of Peter the Great early in the eighteenth century was the decisive influence of the Church on the national mentality challenged.

There is debate among historians both as to the degree to which Peter the Great set Russia on a new path by his numerous and sweeping reforms and whether these reforms constituted the coherent implementation of a premeditated plan, on the one hand, or a piecemeal response to the exigencies of the wars he waged, on the other. Certainly Western influences had begun to percolate into Muscovy under Peter's father, Tsar Alexis, in the second half of the seventeenth century and even earlier, as attested by the appearance at court of Western coaches and clocks. At the same time it is indisputable that under Peter Russia became a European power and began to seek in Western civilization the means with which to sustain and enhance its new status. As a result of the Great Northern War against Sweden, Russia acquired territory on the Baltic littoral, gained access to the Baltic Sea and, in 1703, laid the foundations for a new capital, St Petersburg, on the desolate, inhospitable banks of the River Neva. The army was reorganized on Western lines, equipped with new weaponry such as flintlocks and bayonets, and drilled in modern fighting techniques. A naval fleet was constructed first in shipyards on the Don with a view to fighting the Turks in the Sea of Azov and then in the Baltic. The Russian administration was reorganized by the creation of 'colleges' on Swedish and Prussian models with the role of supervising areas of activity such as foreign relations, state revenue and expenditure, the army, the navy, commerce and justice, and by the establishment of a Senate intended in the first instance to oversee government during Peter's absences. The Church was subordinated to the state, first through the suspension of the Patriarchate on the death of Patriarch Adrian in 1700 and then through the foundation in 1721 of a Holy Synod by means of which the secular ruler could control ecclesiastical affairs. Many steps were taken to divert the wealth of the Church to the state. Industry was stimulated, initially with a view to military applications in ship-building, the manufacture of munitions and provision of sail-cloth and uniforms (though later in Peter's reign production of such materials as bricks, glass, china, silk and velvet increased). Educational institutions were founded, including a navigation school, an engineering academy and an artillery academy. An edict of 1714 required that the children of all landowners and civil servants between the ages of ten and fifteen receive an elementary education (though the results were disappointing, owing not least to the resistance of the nobility to the measure). An Academy of Sciences was opened in 1725 shortly after Peter's death. The Western Julian calendar was introduced in 1700, the first Russian newspaper was produced in 1703, a simplified orthography was introduced in the years 1708–10 in order to make the written word more widely accessible, many foreign books, mainly of a technical nature and informative value, were translated into Russian, and numerous foreign experts – notably military men, engineers and architects – were attracted to Russia [32; 47].

It is doubtful whether Peter's reforms, far-reaching as they were, penetrated deeply. Throughout the eighteenth century Western civilization affected mainly the court and sections of the nobility, and in the second half of the century several writers mocked the formal, artificial character of attempts to impose it. Nevertheless the importance of Peter's reforms for subsequent generations, and in particular both for the state and its opponents in nineteenth-century Russia, can hardly be exaggerated. (The tendency to view Peter as bringing about a decisive change in Russia's destiny – whether one considered that change as for the better or for the worse – is attested by his prominence in the debates of nineteenth-century thinkers.) Subsequent rulers did not abandon Peter's ambition to make of Russia a powerful, expanding European empire. Nor did they seek to dismantle the sort of state – secular, centralized, militaristic, oppressive – that Peter bequeathed. At the same time Peter created the conditions in which enlightenment, science, and a secular culture could develop. If in the reign of Peter himself Westernization took the form principally of military, administrative, technological and economic change, in following reigns, and particularly in the reign of Catherine II, it took cultural forms, finding expression in the work of Western architects (especially in St Petersburg), the development of a Western style of painting, the introduction of French theatre and Italian opera and the flowering of journalism and imaginative literature. The poets and dramatists – Kantemir, Lomonosov, Sumarokov, Fonvizin, Derzhavin – who in the eighteenth century begin to create *ab ovo* a literature of a Western sort are in a sense products of Peter's reform and in most cases revere him and consciously commend his project [59].

THE INTELLIGENTSIA

The post-Petrine state, in order to continue to compete effectively with the Western European powers with which Peter had brought Russia into closer contact, required men versed in Western skills: administrative, judicial, and technological as well as military. Thus from the middle of the century small numbers of young men were sent abroad to study in Western institutions. (The scientist and poet Lomonosov, who studied at Marburg and Freiburg in the years 1736–41, is an outstanding early example.) However, the state had no means of ensuring that the young Russian nobleman abroad acquired only knowledge that would be of practical use to the authorities on his return. He might also imbibe, in eighteenth-century Europe, ideas that would in the long term prove deeply damaging to the Russian political and social order. Thus Radishchev, sent by Catherine II to Leipzig in the 1760s to study law, developed an interest in such notions as the social contract, natural law and the separation of the powers, which led him to abhor the institutions of autocracy and serfdom [*Doc. 1*]. These notions, which helped to undermine the *ancien régime* in France, found expression in Radishchev's famous critique of the Russian political and social system, *A Journey from St Petersburg to Moscow* (1790) [25; 111; 112]. Thus from the late eighteenth century a section of the educated class began to turn into a source of opposition to the state which, in the wake of Peter's Westernization and in the interests of the further modernization of the country, had helped to bring that class into being. By the 1840s this section of the population had crystallized into a grouping which became known as the intelligentsia.

The salient characteristics of the Russian intelligentsia, most would agree, have until very recent times included the following. Firstly, the intelligentsia does not subscribe to the set of values promoted by the autocratic – or later totalitarian – state but has a capacity for independent thought; it is a 'critically thinking minority', to use the phrase of the revolutionary Populist Lavrov (see pp. 68–70). Secondly, it is bound as a result of this independence to find itself in some form of opposition – philosophical, cultural, moral, religious, ultimately political – to the authorities; for in a society in which the state attempts to impose monolithic values, as was the case in tsarist Russia as well as the Soviet Union, pluralism is necessarily more or less subversive and intolerable. Thirdly, since the intelligentsia is an oppositional force, it is at best, in a phrase used recently by the Soviet dissident Siniavsky, 'separated from power'. The consequences of this separation are arguably far-reaching. One might attribute to it a refreshing or inspiring idealism and freedom from corruption. Equally one might see it as the cause of unpracticality, even an irresponsible tendency to advocate economic, social and political solutions to problems that will not have to be tested in reality by members of the intelligentsia themselves. Fourthly, it also follows from the fact that the intelligentsia plays an oppositional role that a willingness to suffer for convictions – the word 'convictions', denoting ideas very strongly held, is to be preferred to the weaker 'beliefs' – is a further defining attribute of the grouping. Members of the intelligentsia, even the more moderate among them, have chosen a path on which they will very probably come into conflict with the authorities and suffer persecution for their dissidence, if we may use the twentieth-century term. In the period with which we are concerned in this book, persecution took many forms. In many instances the persecution was relatively mild (for example, the declaration by the authorities that Chaadaev was insane, dispatch of the troublesome poet Lermontov to the Caucasian front-line and exile of the novelist Turgenev to his country estate). In other cases, though, the authorities resorted to more draconian measures such as imprisonment and Siberian exile, as meted out to Dostoevsky and Chernyshevsky, and – in relatively rare cases of armed mutiny and acts of terrorism – execution as suffered by five of the Decembrists in 1826 and members of The People's Will in the 1880s.

PART TWO: PHASES OF OPPOSITION

3 THE AGE OF ALEXANDER I (1801–25)

THE 'FINE BEGINNING OF ALEXANDER'S DAYS'

The seeds of the intellectual and political dissent that was eventually to turn into revolt and carry away Russian autocracy in 1917 are to be found in the second half of the eighteenth century. It was then, in the age of Catherine II, that elements of the nobility, despite their enthusiasm for imperial expansion, began to question the degree to which Russian absolutism was enlightened, to speculate on the duties of rulers, to test the limits of freedom of expression and to lay down moral obligations for their class. This tendency is to some extent apparent in the poetry of Derzhavin and notably so in the drama of Sumarokov, Fonvizin and Kniazhnin and in Radishchev's *Journey from St Petersburg to Moscow* (see p. 10). Such seeds of dissent, however, did not immediately germinate; indeed the first fifteen years of the nineteenth century are not on the whole notable for opposition to autocracy but rather for a sense of optimism and national unity and for conservative rather than radical thought.

The sense of optimism at the beginning of the century (captured in Pushkin's phrase which stands at the head of this section) is explained partly by the fact that Alexander I – who came to power as a result of a palace coup in which his father Paul, Catherine's despised son, was murdered – gave signs in the early years of his reign of being receptive to the opinions of others and of wishing to dispense with tyrannical methods of government. Tutored in his youth by La Harpe, a Swiss devotee of contemporary radical French doctrines, Alexander was alive to the abuses of the Russian administration and before his accession flirted with the idea of establishing a constitution and handing over power to representative government. In 1802–3, together with an 'unofficial committee' consisting of four friends of long standing (N. N. Novosiltsev, Count Paul Stroganov, Count Kochubei and the Polish Prince Adam Czartoryski), Alexander discussed the problem of serfdom (though this discussion yielded no substantial results) and the machinery of government. Dissent ceased to be arbitrarily crushed, censorship was relaxed, and the periodical press and book printing suddenly expanded [*45 pp. 69–83*]. One of the dominant statesmen of the first half of Alexander's reign, Speransky, attempted to reform the bureaucracy [41]. The sense of national unity in the early part of the nineteenth century is explained by the country's preoccupation with the war against Napoleon and in particular by the effort required to repel the invasion of 1812 and by pride in the success of that effort. The mood of this period is captured by the idealistic patriotic journalist Sergei Glinka, who hoped the resistance to Napoleon might produce a moral awakening in the nobility and lead to social transformation [*95 pp. 73–84*]. The institution of autocracy was defended by Karamzin, the leading man of letters of the period, as essential to Russia's well-being. In his *Memoir on Ancient and Modern Russia*, written in 1810–11, Karamzin warned of the danger of tampering with existing political structures and advised against constitutional experiments of the sort with which Alexander had been toying [16]. Karamzin's celebrated *History of the Russian State*, the first eight volumes of which were published in 1818, represented a further defence of the autocratic state in Russia [83; *92 ch. 6*]. And yet in retrospect we may see a potential threat to the autocracy even in the conservative thought of the Alexandrine period. For the Russian state, after Peter the Great, was in a sense a revolutionary state that set out to uproot tradition and Westernize Russia, and as such it courted opposition from one stream of conservative thinkers. Thus Shishkov, suspicious of Enlightenment values and intellectual cosmopolitanism, which he viewed as causes of revolutionary upheaval, regarded Alexander with distrust as a ruler prone to dangerous foreign innovation. Nations, Shishkov believed, should remain faithful to their own traditions; Russia should therefore seek its identity in pre-Petrine Muscovy, in a supposed golden age of pure rustic morals [*95 ch. 1*].

THE DECEMBRIST REVOLT

In the years after the victory over Napoleon a mystical conservatism came to the fore in Alexander and supplanted the apparent liberal leanings of the earlier part of his reign. Russia joined the Holy Alliance which after the Congress of Vienna dedicated itself to the preservation of the great monarchic states in Europe. A crude military man, Arakcheev, a parade-ground disciplinarian who had once served Alexander's father Paul, replaced Speransky as the Emperor's most influential adviser. Magnitsky and Runich, notorious for their imposition of religious and moral correctness on the Universities of Kazan in 1819, and St Petersburg in 1821, respectively, gained influence in educational administration and helped to create a climate in which it was difficult to spread enlightenment. Whereas previously Alexander had entertained views radical for the time, now his political confidants included converts to a religious 'awakening' who sought personal communion with God, such as Prince Golitsyn, the acting Minister of Education from 1816, and the conservative diplomat Aleksandr Sturdza, son of a Moldavian father and a Greek mother, for whom the Holy Alliance represented a utopian league of Christian states capable of restoring religion as a basis for national identity [95 *ch. 7*].

In this climate disenchantment quickly took hold in the educated class, particularly among that military, social and intellectual elite which through service in the conquering Russian army had had first-hand experience of life in the West during the campaigns of the Napoleonic Wars. The causes of this disenchantment, which culminated in the revolt of December 1825 by certain army regiments and which were described by the Decembrists themselves, as these mutineers were retrospectively called, in their subsequent depositions to the commission set up to investigate the revolt, were numerous and deep [*Doc. 2*] [26 *pp. 32–57*]. The education of the Russian nobleman of the generation to which the Decembrists belonged had cultivated a consciousness of obligations as well as rights and had illustrated the concept of civic responsibility with heroic examples from classical antiquity. The quest for moral perfection and a philanthropic concern for one's fellow human beings were further encouraged by Free-masonry, attractive to many educated Russians from the age of Catherine. (Many of the Decembrists were former Masons; some of them had been initiated in Paris.) Moreover, as a result of the Napoleonic Wars these noblemen became acquainted with the current intellectual ferment in the West and with liberal writings such as those of the Franco-Swiss novelist and political journalist Benjamin Constant. They became aware too of the existence of such partially representative political institutions as the British House of Commons. It was in any case a period of Romantic artistic revolt and political rebellion in Europe: poets exalted the gifted individual striving for self-fulfilment in spite of the dead-weight of custom and radical groups – for example the Spanish soldiers led by Riego y Núñez in the revolt of 1820 – and even whole peoples, such as the Greeks and South American colonists led by Simón Bolívar, began to rebel against monarchy and empire. In several countries patriotic secret societies sprang up, such as the Tugendbund (a 'society for virtue' dedicated to the moral regeneration of Germany), the Carbonari (opponents of the conservative regimes imposed on Italy after the Napoleonic Wars), and the Philiki Etaireia, led by Ypsilantis, a Greek soldier in Russian service who in 1821 launched an abortive invasion of Moldavia in the hope of eventually liberating the Balkans from Turkish rule.

The increased familiarity of educated Russians with conditions abroad and the political climate, movements and organizations which these Russians encountered there threw the oppressiveness of Russian society into sharp relief. Pride in the victory over Napoleon quickly turned to despair at the realization that Russia was unworthy – or so the words and actions of the tsar led these noblemen to believe – to enjoy the fruits of the revolutionary and Napoleonic period that were being granted to other European peoples. It was noted with bitterness in Russia that the laws and institutions of Finland had been respected when it became a Grand Duchy of Russia in 1809; that a constitutional monarchy had been set up in the defeated country, France; that a constitutional charter, providing for a bicameral parliament, was granted to the truncated kingdom of Poland and that in the speech with which he opened the Polish Sejm in 1818 Alexander vaguely suggested the extension of a similar political system to Russia; and that the German serfs in the Baltic provinces had been liberated, albeit without land, in 1811, 1817 and 1819. At the same time the tsar made disparaging remarks about Russians and seemed to favour the opinions of foreigners. Aided by his brothers Constantine, Nicholas and Michael, he indulged the 'paradomania' characteristic of his family, having his army remorselessly drilled and having trivial errors and misdemeanours brutally punished. Notorious military colonies were set up in which soldiers would simultaneously train and work the land. Thus dissatisfaction among the noblemen reflected wounded national pride and resentment at domestic repression as well as attraction to alien ideas.

The dissatisfaction found expression in several forms and groupings almost as soon as the Napoleonic Wars had ended and the Congress of Vienna had decreed the new European order. Various political societies sprang up in Russia too, their organization and rituals owing much to their founders' familiarity with the practices of Masonic lodges. As early as 1816 General Orlov had mused about the possibility of creating a somewhat romantic 'Order of Russian Knights'. In the same year a Union of Salvation was founded by a number of Guards officers (Aleksandr Muraviov, Nikita Muraviov, the brothers Matvei and Sergei Muraviov-Apostol, Prince Trubetskoi and Iakushkin; these men were later joined by Pestel). The goals of the Union included the establishment of a constitutional monarchy and the abolition of serfdom. In 1817 a constitution was drawn up for it which envisaged different degrees of initiation as in a Masonic lodge. By 1818 the society had been dissolved but in its place a new society was set up in Moscow under the name Union of Welfare, with objectives that were primarily moral and social rather than political. A further constitution, known as the Green Book and modelled on that of the Tugendbund, was compiled for the new Union. This constitution placed emphasis – just as men of the previous generation, formed in the eighteenth century, might have done – on the duty of members to unite the forces of virtue against vice, spread rules of morality and enlightenment, perform philanthropic works, educate their fellows, promote justice, and help to stimulate the national economy [26 *pp.* 69–99]. These aims were to be achieved within the existing political framework by means of both social activity and personal example.

Soon the Union of Welfare too was dissolved, partly because news had been received that the authorities were aware of its existence but also because of tensions within the Union which came to the surface at a conference held in Moscow in 1821. Out of the Union, however, there arose two new groupings. One grouping, the so-called Northern Society, was based in St Petersburg and had some support in Moscow. The Northern Society was headed from 1823 by Nikita Muraviov, Prince Obolensky and Prince Trubetskoi; the civic poet Ryleev, who joined it in 1823, also became influential in it [78]. The other grouping, a more radical Southern Society, was located among troops stationed in the Ukraine, in Tulchin. The Southern Society was led by Pestel, the dominating figure among the Decembrists. Son of the governor-general of Siberia, Pestel had been educated for four years in Germany and subsequently wounded at the Battle of Borodino in 1812. The Southern Society was swollen by the arrival of former officers of the Semionovsky Guards Regiment which had been disbanded after mutinying in 1820 in protest at the severity of a new commanding officer. In 1821 a further group, the Society of the United Slavs, was founded by the brothers Andrei and Piotr Borisov and Liublinsky among middle-ranking officers of the lower nobility stationed in Leshchin, close to Vasilkov where there was a branch of the Southern Society. In 1825 this Society fused with the socially and intellectually more powerful Southern Society. There were tensions between the Northern and Southern Societies which foredoomed the action they eventually took. In particular Pestel was unable to persuade the Northern Society of the need for regicide, possibly to be carried out by a *garde perdue* of assassins, and for a period of revolutionary dictatorship by a provisional government. Vague plots were hatched by the Southern Society to kidnap or assassinate the tsar or stage a mutiny.

Eventually the dissatisfaction of the various groups found expression in a disastrously ill-planned way in December 1825 in the confused situation that followed the sudden death of Alexander on 19 November in Taganrog on the Sea of Azov. On 27 November an oath of allegiance had been taken to Alexander's eldest surviving brother Constantine, whose reputation for liberalism – largely undeserved – made him a more popular choice as ruler than his younger brother Nicholas. However, Constantine, having contracted a morganatic marriage to a Catholic Polish noble lady, had previously agreed to renounce his claim to the throne and now declined to accept it. On 14 December arrangements in due course proceeded for the swearing of the oath of allegiance to Nicholas. While members of government institutions and most regiments complied, mutinous officers of the Northern Society led some 3,000 men into Senate Square in St Petersburg where they stood indecisively throughout the day. The revolt was disadvantaged by the fact that Prince Trubetskoi, who it had been decided should serve as temporary dictator, took refuge in the Austrian embassy. The military commander of St Petersburg, General Miloradovich, tried to persuade the mutineers to disperse but he was shot dead by an officer named Kakhovsky. Further attempts at intercession were made by the Metropolitan Serafim and the Grand Duke Michael. Towards evening loyal troops who had surrounded the mutineers opened fire with cannon and the mutineers scattered. Sections of the army in the South, led by Bestuzhev-Riumin and Sergei Muraviov-Apostol, prominent members of the Southern Society, revolted when news of the mutiny in St Petersburg reached them, but they were soon defeated by forces loyal to the regime. All the leaders of both societies were quickly arrested and a lengthy investigation, in which Nicholas himself took part, was carried out. On 13 July 1826 five of the Decembrists – Bestuzhev-Riumin, Kakhovsky, Sergei Muraviov-Apostol, Pestel, and Ryleev – were hanged in the Peter and Paul Fortress, a further 116 were sentenced to various terms of hard labour and exile or service in disciplinary battalions and some 300 more were disciplined in less severe ways [26; 77; 78; 79]

The Decembrists were no more united in terms of political thought than they were cohesive as a political organization. The divergent political stances of the Northern and Southern Societies are most clearly represented by the two major political statements formulated by Decembrists, Nikita Muraviov's draft of a constitution and Pestel's incomplete project *Russian Law*, drafted over the period 1821–25. Both documents are extant in two versions. Pestel's title consciously echoes that of the first Russian legal code drawn up in the eleventh century. Muraviov, who begins his first draft with a critique of the arbitrariness of autocracy [*Doc. 3*], aims at the establishment of a constitutional monarchy in which the people will be the source of sovereign power. All Russians will be equal before the law and will have the remedy of *habeas corpus* against arbitrary detention. There will be trial by jury. Serfdom will be abolished, as will the detested military colonies. Peasants' homes, gardens, implements and cattle will be recognized as their own property, but the landowners' lands will remain in their possession. People will be free to choose their own trade and practise their religion. Muraviov conceives regional assemblies as a bulwark against the potentially oppressive centralized state and advocates federalism on the American model, envisaging the division of Russia into thirteen states and two regions, each with its own legislative assembly. Only decisions affecting the state as a whole will be taken by the legislative assembly in the capital. That assembly will be bicameral, consisting of a Sovereign Duma of forty-two members (who must fulfil a property qualification) elected by the governing institutions of the states and regions, and a Chamber of Representatives (one for every 50,000 male inhabitants) elected for two years by the citizens of the states and regions [20 *pp. 42–50*; 26 *pp. 103–18*].

Pestel, on the other hand, envisages a centralized republic on the French revolutionary model. He conceives his *Russian Law* as a statement of the mutual obligations and rights of government and people, a code setting out the principles on which a new political and social order will be based, the principal changes that need to be made, and the necessary transitional measures. The *Russian Law* is both a blueprint for the 'Provisional Supreme Administration' that will replace the existing government and a charter for the people, informing them of the programme to be implemented. Government, in Pestel's eyes, exists for the sole purpose of promoting the good of the people, all the people. Serfdom and the military colonies, noble status, and differences between estates are to be abolished. For Pestel, himself a dictatorial personality who apparently regarded the people as a characterless mass to be moulded at will by the government, society is divided into those who command and those who obey. The common weal takes precedence over private happiness. Although Pestel advocates freedom in economic matters and outlines an electoral system, he is in essence authoritarian and *Realpolitik* prevails. Small nations are to be submerged politically and culturally by larger ones. Non-Russian minorities inhabiting actual parts of the Empire such as Finland or regions on which Pestel had designs, such as Moldavia and the Caucasus, would be Russified. Although the *Russian Law* proclaimed religious tolerance, acts of members of non-Christian faiths which are deemed contrary to the spirit of Christian law will be prohibited. Despite a pledge to maintain freedom of the press, all societies were to be banned. A secret political police was to watch for signs of subversive activity. Even the size of townships, as seats of bad morality, should be regulated (a town should accommodate no more than 10,000 males). Pestel vehemently rejects the federal model of the state favoured by Muraviov, arguing – as Catherine II had done – that such a model is particularly inappropriate in a country so vast and embracing such diverse peoples as Russia [*Doc. 4*] [*20 pp. 51–8; 26 pp. 124–56*].

The Decembrist Revolt failed to achieve any softening of autocratic government; indeed it is arguable that it made Nicholas's regime even harsher than it might otherwise have been. And yet the revolt was a new departure, differing markedly from the palace *coups* by which Catherine II and Alexander I had come to the throne. It was also an important landmark: for it was to serve as a source of inspiration to opponents of autocracy as a selfless and patriotic attempt to mitigate the severity of Russia's political and social system (and also to restore its economy after the ruinous period of war). Moreover, the harsh treatment of leading participants in the revolt, far from deterring emulation of their actions, laid the foundations for a powerful martyrology which sanctified their memory. Pushkin penned an epistle in verse to the conspirators sentenced to Siberian exile in which he looked forward to the time when their fetters would fall away and Freedom would greet them at the door of their prison. Most importantly, the revolt can be seen in retrospect as a starting point in the history of more or less organized rebellion against autocracy in Russia. Of course, there was no attempt as yet to couple the reasoned discontentment of sections of the nobility with the elemental rebelliousness of the peasantry which had periodically erupted in large-scale uprisings (see p. 5) and which continued to find regular expression in small-scale local *jacqueries*. Nevertheless the Decembrists, for all the variety of their opinions and their confusion over objectives, may in retrospect be seen as having taken the first step on the path that led by way of further ill-thought-out conspiracies in the 1840s and 1860s to the revolutionary movement which began to unfold with greater force in the 1870s and which eventually, when the country had been weakened by social transformation and military defeat, was to topple autocracy in 1917.

4 THE AGE OF NICHOLAS I (1825–55)

RUSSIAN CULTURE IN THE AGE OF NICHOLAS

The reign of Nicholas I is among the most repressive periods of nineteenth-century Russian history. The tsar himself, most at home on the parade-ground and among military men, had no interest in or sympathy with liberal or radical ideas. He was a staunch defender of established power and in 1849 sent Russian troops to support the Habsburg monarchy in the face of the Hungarian revolt. His instinctive belief in the legitimacy of autocratic power, coupled with a determination to prevent any recurrence of a mutiny like that of the Decembrists, inspired the introduction of measures designed to restrict freedom of expression and to root out dissent. A new censorship law was introduced in 1826, by Shishkov, now Minister of Education, which was so harsh that one censor complained that even the Lord's Prayer could now be interpreted as a Jacobin speech [95 p. 200]. The law was repealed in 1828, but by 1848 there were no fewer than twelve censorship agencies. Even if a work was passed by the censor the author or publisher could be punished if on publication it displeased the tsar or some highly placed personage [54 p. 44]. Censorship was a factor of which all writers and thinkers in Nicholas's reign had to take account, sometimes with bizarre results: a censor objected, for example, to the title of Gogol's novel, *Dead Souls* on the grounds that souls were immortal. The Third Department (of the Emperor's Own Chancery), established in 1826 and headed until 1844 by Count Benckendorff, was given responsibility for political security, supervision of politically suspicious persons, sectarians and foreign subjects and even for theatre censorship [46]. At the same time the state itself promoted an ideology of its own in the form of the doctrine of Official Nationality, which was promulgated in 1833 by the Minister of Education, Count Uvarov, and which was based on defence of the three principles of autocracy, Orthodoxy and nationality [60]. The age of Nicholas is therefore associated by writers and thinkers with reaction, stagnation, the surveillance of subjects by government and fellow subjects, and attempts to crush independent thought [57]. The regime became particularly severe in the last seven years of Nicholas's reign (1848–55), a period that came to be described as the 'dismal seven years' (*mrachnoe semiletie*), during which Nicholas sought to shore up Russia's defences against revolutionary forces of the sort that had been unleashed in many Western European countries in 1848–49.

Paradoxical as it may seem, given the pains taken by the government to stifle the free spirit, the repressive Nicholaevan age is notable for the formation of an independent intelligentsia in the sense in which it was defined above (see pp. 9–11) and for a marvellous intellectual awakening that reached its apogee in the 1840s, an awakening subsequently described in a rich memoir literature [1; 14]. This energy found expression in both the formation of a strong native tradition of thought and the flowering of an imaginative literature inextricably bound up with the development of philosophical, social and political ideas. Pushkin, whose poetry is of seminal importance in this literature, produced most of his work in the reign of Nicholas and the poet and prose writer Lermontov and the novelist, short-story writer and dramatist Gogol all of theirs in this period. The novelists Goncharov, Turgenev, Dostoevsky and Tolstoy, the satirist Saltykov (who wrote under the pseudonym Shchedrin) and the poet Nekrasov all began their literary careers in this reign too. The nature of the regime and the oppressive conditions under which these writers laboured created a sense of high purpose and civic duty in the artist. Many writers came to feel an obligation, as the historian of Russian literature D. S. Mirsky has put it, to choose

subjects exclusively from contemporary or almost contemporary Russian life... The novelists were expected to react, sensitively and significantly, to the current life of the nation. Partly owing to the severity of the censorship for other branches of literature, fiction, from the forties onward, became an important and widely listened-to mouthpiece of social thinking, and the critics demanded that every time a novelist gave his work to the world it should contain things worth meditating on and worth analysing from the point of view of the social issues of the day. As a rule, the novelists took the obligation very seriously, and never ignored it, at least in their more ambitious work. This 'social' ... or 'civic' ... colouring is a general characteristic of the European novel of the mid nineteenth century, but it is nowhere more apparent than in Russia. [56 *p. 172*]

The sense of social responsibility among Russian writers helps to explain their leaning in the middle of the century towards Realism and their tendency to abandon poetry in favour of prose, and in particular the novel, as the most suitable vehicle for the depiction of individual destinies against a larger social backcloth [51]. However, beyond its function as a vehicle for examination of issues which could not be adequately discussed in other ways, imaginative literature in nineteenth-century Russia acquired a deeper, moral significance as an expression of the free conscience under authoritarian rule. It represented light, movement and life against a background of darkness, immobility and death (images frequently used to evoke the conditions of Nicholaevan Russia). Indeed its tenacity was a sign that the nation, for all its suffering, was nevertheless stirring and might yet have a vigorous and independent, though still enigmatic, future. This possibility is famously evoked in the closing passage of the first part of Gogol's novel *Dead Souls*, in which the troika of Gogol's anti-hero Chichikov is transmuted into an image of Russia herself, flying through the air, 'full of divine inspiration':

> Russia, where are you flying to? Answer! She gives no answer. The bells fill the air with their wonderful tinkling; the air is torn asunder, it thunders and is transformed into wind; everything on earth is flying past, and, looking askance, other nations and states draw aside and make way for her.

If the regime of Nicholas did not in fact stifle creative energy it did however have the effect of driving idealistic members of the educated class to seek fulfilment in an other-worldly realm. This realm was not one sought by the devotees of established religion but one to which philosophy and the arts, particularly poetry, seemed in the Romantic age to offer access. We do not yet find in Russian thought in the age of Nicholas a concern or explicit engagement with concrete practical issues in the fields of law, economics or sociology, let alone politics. This state of affairs is not explicable primarily as a product of the existence of censorship. Rather it is due to the fact that the intelligent individual fired by civic concern, denied the channels open to such people in the West – for example, politics, the Church, science, the professions, the local public service of the gentleman – took refuge in art, aesthetics, metaphysics and philosophy of history. Here the idealistic self sought communion with the supra-rational absolutes of German Romantic philosophy or, more destructively, plunged into the self-analysis characteristic of the 'superfluous man' so commonly portrayed in the imaginative literature of the age.

CHAADAEV'S 'PHILOSOPHICAL LETTER'

An examination of the stirrings of opposition to autocracy in the reign of Nicholas I must begin with discussion of the so-called 'Philosophical Letter' written by Chaadaev, a *habitué* of the aristocratic salons of Moscow in which intellectual life was principally conducted in the late 1820s. Chaadaev, who had travelled in the West in the period 1823–26, wrote the letter in 1829 but it was not published until 1836, whereupon the journal in which it had appeared, *The Telescope (Teleskop)*, was promptly closed by the authorities. The first of a cycle of eight letters, but the only one to be published in Chaadaev's lifetime, the 'Philosophical Letter' is important above all in two respects. Firstly, in comparing the histories and civilizations of Russia and the West – a comparison which for Chaadaev is catastrophically disadvantageous to Russia – the letter establishes a framework for debate about Russia's shortcomings for at least the remainder of the reign of Nicholas. Secondly, it challenges the official optimism of a regime confident of Russia's military might in the post-Napoleonic world and of its own domestic security now that the Decembrist Revolt had been crushed and repressive measures taken. Chaadaev's letter fundamentally questions the values enshrined in Official Nationality and the historical destiny to which Count Benckendorff laid claim in his famous boast that Russia's past was 'admirable', her present 'more than magnificent' and her future 'beyond the grasp of the most daring imagination' [quoted in 34 ii, *p.* 799]. To supporters of the established order the letter seemed so threatening, indeed perverse, that Chaadaev was declared insane and confined to house arrest and a doctor was instructed to visit him. To opponents of the regime, on the other hand, the letter – in Herzen's famous phrase – seemed like a 'shot that rang out in the dark night' [14 ii, *p.* 516].

Chaadaev excludes the Russians from membership of the group of peoples who have exerted a beneficial influence on human civilization. This slight is implicit in Chaadaev's reference to Moscow, the place where the letter was written, as 'Necropolis' ('the city of the dead' in Greek) and in the fact that the letter is written not in Russian but in French, as if the Russians do not themselves possess a language suitable as a vehicle for historical and philosophical discourse. However, the slight is also explicit. The Russians, Chaadaev boldly asserts, have contributed no universal idea or great truth to the common stock of human experience. They stand outside 'the great human families', belonging neither to the West nor to the East. Their culture is superficial and imitative. They live outside time, inhabiting only a narrow kind of present, without a past or future. Their history is a series of random events without inner development or natural progression. Since a people with no history has no fixed points, they live in a moral void, indifferent to good and evil, truth and falsehood. They resemble the nomads who throughout early Russian history roamed their steppes or – we might add – the 'superfluous man' of the literature of the Nicholaevan age; indeed Chaadaev himself may have provided one of Pushkin's models for his character Eugene Onegin.

Chaadaev contends that the 'whole history of modern society occurs on the level of beliefs'; interests 'have always been provoked by beliefs, never the other way around'; all political revolutions have in essence been moral revolutions. Given the paramountcy of the moral and spiritual life of a people, as of an individual, over the intellectual or material, the supposed superiority of the Western forms of Christianity to Russian Orthodoxy has grim implications for the Russians. In the West – to which Chaadaev attributed a unity that transcended the ethnic, linguistic and cultural divisions among the Western peoples – the Catholic Church had helped to diffuse the ideas of justice, duty, law and order. Russia, on the other hand, has laboured under 'crude superstition'. Significantly, it is from the Latin form of the Lord's Prayer that Chaadaev draws the epigraph which guides the reader at the beginning of the letter: *Adveniat regnum tuum* ('Thy kingdom come').

In several respects Chaadaev's 'letter' reflects preoccupations of Western European culture during the Romantic period when interest in the national distinctiveness of individual peoples was supplanting the more cosmopolitan outlook of the eighteenth-century Enlightenment. Chaadaev shows greater interest in the Christian Middle Ages than in pagan antiquity. He believes the masses are 'subject to certain forces located at the summit of society', that is to say the 'thinkers' who 'provide an impetus for the collective intelligence of the nation' such as the druids, skalds and bards of the primitive Celts, Scandinavians and Germans respectively. And yet just at the time when other European peoples, such as the Czechs, the Serbs and the Magyars, were beginning to explore aspects of their culture – language, oral poetry, folk music, myths, religion, history, costume – that revealed their distinctiveness, Chaadaev was underlining the Russians' lack of a sharply defined collective personality. Subsequently Chaadaev offered a partial recantation in his 'Apology of a Madman'. The fate awaiting the Russian people as it is presented in the 'Philosophical Letter', however, is bleak indeed: the Russians could not assimilate 'at a stroke' all of the progress so slowly made by the peoples of Europe under the influence of their religion and seemed to exist 'only to serve as a great lesson to the world' [*Doc. 5*] [5; 20 *pp. 67–78*; 80; 81; 82].

SLAVOPHILISM

Chaadaev's 'Philosophical Letter' both stimulated debate about the relationship between Russia and the West and helped to determine the position adopted in that debate by one group of participants in it, the so-called Slavophiles, who in the early 1840s began to express their views through the journal *The Muscovite (Moskvitianin)*. Stung by Chaadaev's dismissal of the Russians as actors on the stage of world history and also by other negative depictions of Russia such as that contained in a book, *Russia in 1839*, written by an aristocratic French traveller, the Marquis de Custine [8], the Slavophiles offered a glowing reappraisal of Russian history and culture and a correspondingly scathing critique of Western civilization. And yet even they, as Romantic conservatives defending native values, could not help finding themselves in opposition to the Nicholaevan state, if not to the institution of autocracy as such, inasmuch as they yearned for a return to the supposedly idyllic pre-Petrine way of life of medieval Muscovy conjured up in the imagination of Alexandrine conservatives such as Shishkov and Sturdza (see pp. 13–14).

The Slavophiles – the most important of whom are the brothers Ivan and Konstantin Aksakov, Khomiakov, the brothers Ivan and Piotr Kireevsky, and Samarin – did not represent an intellectual group expressing more or less unanimous views, still less did they resemble an organized political party. Rather they were a collection of individuals with a shared affection for the way of life and traditions of rural Russia and a common antipathy to the rationalism, materialism, individualism, egoism, atheism, spiritual breakdown and social fragmentation which they believed a continuing influx of Western ideas and practices would introduce into their country. Although the Slavophiles opposed serfdom on humanitarian grounds, it might be said of them that they were seeking to preserve an order in which they, as for the most part wealthy members of the landowning nobility, had a vested interest. It should be noted too that in spite of their hostility to what they perceived as the spirit of Western culture they themselves were steeped in that culture. Indeed their search for *narodnost'*, the distinctive character of their own people, whose historical significance Chaadaev had denied, may on the broadest level be seen as part of that general European search for ethnicity, the concept of *Volkstum* advanced by the eighteenth-century German thinker Herder, which was so pronounced in the first half of the nineteenth century.

The Slavophiles' love of things Russian found expression in Konstantin Aksakov's habit of donning Russian national costume (an eccentricity which led to his being mistaken for a Persian) and in his philological investigations, and in Piotr Kireevsky's important collection of Russian folk songs. They gravitated towards Moscow, as the ancient capital, the seat of the Russian patriarchate and of the princes who had thrown off the Tatar yoke. At the same time their antipathy to things Western led them to abhor the newer capital St Petersburg, with its Western architecture and *mores*, and its creator, Peter, who they believed had diverted Russia from its true historical path. They also deplored the materialism, the preoccupation with 'luxury', which had given rise to the development of a 'science of wealth', as Ivan Kireevsky described political economy in his essay of 1852 'On the Nature of European Culture and its Relation to the Culture of Russia', one of the most important expositions of the Slavophile outlook [27 *pp. 202–3*]. They disparaged Roman law, on which many Western legal systems were based, on account of its allegedly dry, legalistic jurisprudence; such law, they believed, revealed an interest in only the external form of justice. (By contrast Khomiakov praised the English legal system which, with its respect for custom and the institution of the jury, seemed to seek justice on a deeper level and to administer the law in a personal and human way.) The spirit of Roman law, Kireevsky argued, informed the codes of honour adopted by the medieval knight, entrenched in his own castle, warring with his neighbours and disputatiously defending his personal interest [27 *pp. 187, 197*].

Central to Slavophilism was a desire to shore up a sense of community which the Slavophiles believed was being lost in the West and which in Russia too would be threatened by further modernization on the Western model. The Slavophiles are with justice seen by the Polish intellectual historian Andrzej Walicki as favouring the more primitive type of society designated by the late nineteenth-century German sociologist Tönnies *Gemeinschaft*, in which relationships are based on kinship and informal ties, as opposed to a society of a more modern kind, designated *Gesellschaft*, in which relationships are regulated on the basis of formal agreement, law and contract [99 *pp. 169–78*]. The group or collectivity therefore has more prominence in their thought than any concern for the individual, or rather they would argue that individuals find fulfilment above all in their harmonious participation in a larger entity. This commitment to the collectivity and a belief that such commitment characterized the Russian people, or perhaps the Slavs in general, and distinguished them from the more individualistic Western peoples, found expression in Slavophilism in various ways.

In the first place, at the lowest level, the individual found protection in the bosom of the family, which the Slavophiles, as wealthy male landowners, conceived in a patriarchal way. The presence of two sets of brothers among their number is itself perhaps indicative of the importance of close family ties in their outlook. (We might add that the father of the Aksakov brothers, Sergei, is himself the author of a work acclaimed in its time, *A Family Chronicle*, a powerful, affectionate depiction of the family life of the landowning gentry in the age of Catherine II.) In the West, on the other hand, the integrity of the family seemed to the Slavophiles to be weakened by the regnant materialism, the promotion of selfish interests and the compartmentalization of life into 'separate aspirations', religious, intellectual, sensual, egoistic and aesthetic [27 *pp. 199–202*].

In the second place, the Slavophiles extolled the *obshchina*, or peasant commune (and in so doing initiated a discussion that was to have considerable importance for various groups within the Russian intelligentsia for the rest of the century). Among the functions of the commune and of the assembly through which the male heads of families discussed their communal affairs was periodic reallocation of the land used by the peasant community in accordance with the changing needs of individual families as they grew or for one reason or another shrank. Interest in this institution was stimulated by a foreign traveller, the Baron von Haxthausen, in a book based on his travels in Russia in 1843, the first two volumes of which appeared in 1847. As a Prussian aristocrat fearful of the disintegration of rural communities, the creation of landless proletariats, the pauperization of the working class and the consequent growth of socialist doctrines, Haxthausen presented the commune which he had discovered in the Russian countryside in paternalistic terms as a protective institution which might shield Russia from these Western ills [*Doc. 8*] [12 i, *pp. 123–35*]. Among mid-nineteenth-century Russian thinkers the origins of the commune came to be heatedly debated. Some saw it as a relatively recent creation of the Russian state, designed to facilitate the gathering of taxes, others as an institution that belonged to a certain stage of historical development in the life of a people which the more advanced Western peoples had long since passed beyond [33 *pp. 508 ff.*]. To the Slavophiles, however, it was an ancient institution which seemed to reflect the non-proprietorial attitude of the Russian peasants towards the land, their unacquisitive nature and their brotherly concern for their fellow human beings. Thus Konstantin Aksakov described it as a 'moral choir' in which individualism was submerged, an active social expression of collective spirit.

In the third place, on a yet broader and higher level than the *obshchina,* stood the Orthodox Church through which the pure Christian spirituality of the Russian people was supposedly manifested and which the Slavophiles sought to show off to its best advantage by its juxtaposition with Roman Catholicism. In the Orthodox Church all were free and equal, whereas the Catholic Church had introduced a spirit of coercion and had organized itself on lines of hierarchy and subordination with the Pope at its head. The Orthodox Church was untainted by involvement in the secular world in which the Pope, as an earthly political figure, had become embroiled. The Orthodox remained faithful to the Christian teachings as established by the early ecumenical councils of the Church held in Nicaea, Constantinople, Ephesus and Chalcedon between the fourth and the eighth centuries, whereas the Western Church, without the consent of the Eastern brethren, had introduced doctrinal change. In particular the Eastern Church objected to the insertion into the Nicene Creed, at Toledo in the sixth century, of the *filioque*, a Latin phrase meaning 'and from the son' by means of which it was asserted that the Holy Ghost proceeds from the Son as well as from the Father. The Orthodox kept in mind the lowly status of rational knowledge by comparison with spiritual understanding, whereas Catholics appeared to set the intellect above the spirit, as attested by the wealth of philosophical and theological enquiry which the Catholic Church had generated. The failings of the Catholic Church – failings shared to some degree by the Protestant Church – pervaded modern Western civilization, with its loss of spirituality and its obsession with the syllogism (a symbol for an exclusively logical, rationalistic view of the world) [*Doc. 11*] [*65 chs 3–4; 97 pp. 127–32, 174–9*].

The contrast between the Eastern and Western Churches is of a piece with the distinction drawn by Khomiakov in his historical writing between on the one hand peoples whom he designates Iranian, whose civilization is informed by the principle of inner freedom and among whom the Slavs are to be included, and on the other hand those whom he designates Kushite, whose organizing principle is compulsion [*97 pp. 67 ff., 91 ff.*]. A similar contrast runs through a memorandum 'On the Internal State of Russia' which Konstantin Aksakov addressed to Alexander II on the accession of the new tsar in the mid-1850s. Unlike the Western peoples the Russians, Aksakov contends, have a non-political nature. They are preoccupied above all with 'moral and communal freedom, the highest aim of which is to achieve a Christian society'; they consequently shun political matters and willingly entrust all authority in the political sphere to the government. Their indifference to political rights and popular government is demonstrated, Aksakov believes, by the assertion in the chronicles that at the dawn of their history the Russians invited the

Varangians to rule over them, and by their decision at the end of the Time of Troubles in the early seventeenth century to choose a new tsar and to submit themselves to him unconditionally. Thus the polity of which the Slavophiles dream is one in which the people are left free by an absolute monarchy to pursue their higher spiritual aims. However, the fundamental principle of the Russian civil order, namely separation of people and state, had been violated by Peter, in whose person the state intruded into the people's lives and customs and forcibly changed their manners and traditions [*Doc. 10*] [20 *pp. 95–107*; 27 *pp. 231–51*]. In a sense, then, even the Slavophiles, for all their conservatism and patriotism, find themselves at odds with the contemporary, repressive, bureaucratic state ruled by a partly Germanic officialdom from a city with a foreign name [84; 85; 86; 91; 93; 99].

LIBERAL WESTERNIZERS

If Slavophilism was more a set of attitudes than a coherent doctrine, Westernism was even more amorphous. The term 'Westernizer' *(zapadnik)* itself, like the term 'Slavophile' *(slavianofil)*, originated as a light-hearted gibe devised by the opposing camp. However, the term embraced a broader, more diverse group of men than the term 'Slavophile'. Indeed even to enumerate the 'Westernizers' of the 1840s and 1850s is not altogether a straightforward task, though one should certainly include the historian Granovsky and the jurist Kavelin; the dilettanti Annenkov and Botkin; the literary critic Belinsky; the future anarchist revolutionary Bakunin; the imaginative writer, essayist and future journalist, political thinker and memoirist Herzen; and even imaginative writers such as the satirist Saltykov, the poet Nekrasov, and the future novelist Turgenev. It is even more difficult to define the beliefs which united the Westernizers than to identify them. To a large extent the Westernizers derived their identity from a shared antipathy to Slavophilism, which they equated with attachment to outmoded tradition, dogma and superstition. Unlike the Slavophiles, the Westernizers revered Peter the Great as the ruler who had given Russia the opportunity to enlighten and civilize itself. Most importantly, they believed that Russia's future well-being depended on respectful study and emulation of the culture, science, way of life and institutions of the superior civilization of the West, where incidentally many of them had studied or travelled extensively [103 *pp. 9–15*].

At the same time any attempt to attribute coherence to Westernism should be qualified by reference to a fissure which began to appear within it in the 1840s and which from the middle of the 1850s was to become as marked as that between Westernism in general, on the one hand, and Slavophilism and later Romantic conservative bodies of thought related to Slavophilism, on the other. One group of Westernizers – especially Granovsky, Botkin, Annenkov, Kavelin and Turgenev among those named above – yearned for limited, gradual, evolutionary change by means of reform initiated and implemented by the autocratic government. These men, the 'men of the 40s' in later parlance, may by virtue of their moderation be described in the Russian context as 'liberals', although they differed from Western liberals (who were more preoccupied with assertion of the rights of the individual and with *laissez-faire* economics) in their reliance on the actions of an authoritarian state. The other group of Westernizers can be seen in retrospect to have consisted in the 1840s of Belinsky, Herzen and Bakunin, men who were prepared to contemplate more far-reaching and even – in the case of Belinsky and Bakunin – bloody revolutionary change. These thinkers, to whom the poet Nekrasov is close, are in a sense forerunners of the socialist 'men of the 60s', such as Chernyshevsky, Dobroliubov and Pisarev (see pp. 55–61).

Of the liberal Westernizers the most important is Granovsky. Through his position as Professor of World History at the University of Moscow throughout the 1840s, and in particular through a celebrated series of public lectures which he delivered in the academic year 1843/44 on the subject of the Frankish Merovingian and Carolingian dynasties (476–751 and 751–887 respectively), Granovsky exercised considerable influence on the nascent Russian public opinion. The study of medieval Western European history yields more to Granovsky than might at first sight seem of obvious interest to the Russian Westernizer of the 1840s. For Granovsky is concerned with the process by which enlightened men – rulers, churchmen, jurists – transformed feudal society by gradually instilling into it spiritual values, humanity, law; in a word, civilization [*Doc. 6*]. Granovsky's moderation finds expression in several ways: for example, in his reluctance altogether to forsake religious belief; in his defence – in a debate among the Westernizers about the French Revolution – of the less extreme faction, the Girondins, in the Legislative Assembly and the National Convention; and in his general advocacy of toleration of viewpoints different from one's own. (It is of interest, however, that Granovsky does not find a satisfactory word in the native lexicon to denote moderation and falls back on a loanword, *moderatsiia*; the most obvious Russian equivalent, *umerennost'*, does not have such uniformly favourable connotations as the English word.) At the same time, Granovsky accepts autocracy as a potential instrument of civilization. He believes that history fulfils some providential idea through the agency of great historical individuals such as Alexander the Great or Peter the Great or even Tamburlaine, and towards the end of his life wrote that Russia in his own day stood in need of Peter's 'stick' [72 *ch.* 3; 103 *ch.* 2; 104].

Granovsky's indulgent, even reverential, view of great rulers is reiterated in an influential essay by his slightly younger contemporary, Kavelin. Entitled 'A Brief Survey of the Juridical Way of Life of Ancient Russia', Kavelin's essay came to be seen as the definitive statement of the Westernist camp on Russian historical development and was opposed as such by the Slavophiles, for whom Samarin offered a detailed rebuttal. Kavelin traced what he saw as the gradual replacement of the patrimonial principle, the principle of family revered by the Slavophiles, by the principle of personality. It was the Muscovite princes, notably Ivan IV, and then Peter the Great, so Kavelin believes, who advanced the principle of personality in Russia, forcing Russians to abandon a patriarchal way of life based on blood relationships and promoting instead notions of a state and a service gentry that transcended family, class or local loyalties. Kavelin's essay contained the germ of the view of the Russian state subsequently propounded by the etatist school of historians, the most notable representative of which was Kavelin's pupil Chicherin (see p. 53). These historians were to argue that in Russia the state was the source of progress and civilization and – perverse as the idea might seem – that it was responsible for the emergence of the individual differentiated from the mass [75 *pp.* 148–51; 103 *ch.* 6]. It is perhaps not surprising, given Russia's backwardness and the political impotence of its small educated public, that Westernizers who feared revolution should have emphasized the active, creative potential of the state and pinned their hopes on an authoritarian ruler, some Alexander the Great or Charlemagne or Peter the Great. However, it must be emphasized that such faith in autocratic power sharply distinguishes Russian 'liberals' of the mid-nineteenth century from Western counterparts who preoccupied themselves with limitation of the role of the state in the lives of individual citizens.

Further important contributions to Westernism, and contributions of similarly moderate character to that of Granovsky, were made by Annenkov and Botkin. Neither Annenkov nor Botkin was himself a writer or thinker of the first rank but both enriched Russian culture in a crucial phase through their writings, their friendship with the major thinkers and the knowledge and first-hand experience of Western lands and art which they gained through their reading and their extensive travels. Annenkov's *Parisian Letters*, which relate to the period from late 1846 to early 1848, betray a striving for detachment, concern to avoid firm commitment to any particular ideology or faction, a sceptical attitude towards the socialist theories then proliferating in France, repugnance at the excesses of the French Revolution and fear of further social upheaval. In correspondence with Marx, Annenkov already expressed fears about the threat posed by communism to some of the achievements of European civilization and to the rights of the individual [103 *ch. 4*].

Of Botkin's writings his *Letters on Spain*, based on a journey to Spain in 1845 and the bulk (six out of seven) of which were published between 1847 and 1849, perhaps most strongly express the spirit of the liberal Westernism of the 1840s. They reveal a love of a foreign land which struck Botkin as colourful and exotic and of a foreign people in whom Botkin detected both an attractive sensualism and a deep religiosity. Spain and its people, moreover, had pertinence for Botkin's compatriots. Living like the Russians on the periphery of Europe and once subjugated by an infidel invader, the Spaniards too were striving to tear themselves away from their past but preserve cherished traditions. Both the Spanish nobleman and the common people exhibited exemplary qualities: in the former Botkin perceived a moral nobility, sense of chivalry and knightly temperament, while in the latter he found a common sense, lucidity and freedom of spirit that might be expected, we may infer, of a people not oppressed by serfdom. Most importantly, Botkin implicitly commended social relationships in Spain. Spaniards' dealings with one another were free and honourable irrespective of differences in social class; the nobleman did not consider it beneath his dignity to mingle with the crowd and the common man was not obsequious towards the nobleman. Clearly such social harmony was desirable for political as well as moral reasons, for it might prevent the development of the antagonisms that lead to revolutionary upheavals [103 *ch. 3*]. We might add that while the equality of social standing that Botkin thought he had found in Spain was clearly absent in pre-reform Russia, a further member of the Westernist circle, Turgenev, seems implicitly to suggest its feasibility there by treating serfs as moral equals of their masters in his *Sportsman's Sketches*, published in the same year as Botkin's *Letters on Spain*.

BELINSKY

Important as the liberal Westernizers were in the creation of a distinctive national culture and the formation of an independent public opinion, they are bound to be overshadowed in any history of opposition to tsarist autocracy by Belinsky, 'furious Vissarion' as he came to be known on account of the passion with which he committed himself to ideas and to Russian literature. Through the force of his combative, proselytizing, suffering personality Belinsky exercised a greater influence than the liberal Westernizers on Russian thought, both in his own time and subsequently. Indeed he stands as a central figure in the nineteenth-century Russian intelligentsia, seeming to embody all its strengths (sincerity, dedication, idealism, seriousness of purpose, and a deep love of literature) and its weaknesses (impetuosity, intolerance, and a tendency to schematic generalization and extremism).

Unlike the majority of his contemporaries in the intelligentsia, Belinsky was not a nobleman. He was the son of a retired naval doctor and the grandson of a priest in rural Russia, where he grew up. He studied at Moscow University from 1829 to 1832, but was expelled before completing his studies, partly it seems for writing a play critical of serfdom. There followed a period of great hardship, which no doubt exacerbated the serious lung disease that had already begun to manifest itself in Belinsky's university years. Belinsky's journalistic career began in 1834 and continued, with short interruptions, until 1848, when he died of consumption at the age of thirty-six. It was during this brief period in the middle of the reign of Nicholas that both a nationally distinctive literature and the intelligentsia itself, as a deracinated social grouping and independent public force, came fully into being in Russia; indeed Belinsky himself presided over and helped to fashion both these developments. He exercised his influence almost exclusively through the medium of literary criticism, which he moulded into much more than a tool for discussion of literature and aesthetics. His essays are appraisals of the artistic merits of works of imaginative literature, to be sure, but they are also both tormented externalizations of his own spiritual crises and free-ranging excursions, apropos of works of art, into such fields as morality, history and society. In the final analysis they take on political significance.

Since Belinsky was a restless spirit incessantly searching for meanings and values which might satisfy him, his ideas were in a constant state of flux and he underwent various *volte-faces*. His career is commonly divided into three main phases (and only in the last phase, it should be emphasized, does his thought have that socially and politically radical character that is posthumously associated with him).

Firstly, in the years 1834–36, under the influence of the German philosopher Schelling, Belinsky is preoccupied with the search for national character as it is reflected – so thinkers of the Romantic period believed – in art. In his dazzling debut, 'Literary Reveries' (1834), he provocatively asserted that Russia as yet had no literature, if by a literature one meant a coherent corpus of works arising out of native soil and expressing the distinctive spirit of a people, *narodnost'*. Nor could Russia yet possess such a literature, because Russian society was too young and had still to liberate itself from Western tutelage [4 *pp. 3–103*]. Art, at this stage of his career, Belinsky sees as an end in itself. The process of artistic creation, discussed in an enthusiastic review of the early stories of Gogol, he regards as a form of clairvoyance: the gifted artist does not so much copy from reality as apprehend the truth in a moment of poetic revelation.

Secondly, in the years 1838–40, intoxicated with the philosophy of Hegel, Belinsky exalts art for its own sake and displays a notorious political conservatism. Following a brief flirtation in 1836 with the philosophy of Fichte, a period of unemployment as a result of the closure of *The Telescope*, for which Belinsky had been writing, and a prolonged bout of illness, Belinsky had sunk in 1837 into a mood of abstract contemplation. With friends such as Konstantin Aksakov, Bakunin and Botkin he now avidly read and debated the works of Hegel, who as Belinsky understood him recognized reality as rational and therefore enabled one to reconcile oneself to one's environment with all its defects. In political terms the reconciliation with reality entailed for Belinsky defence of the divine right of kings and slavish obedience to the state. He advised individuals to renounce their own personality and submit to the universal and general as the only truth and reality and he warned that society would crush anyone who rebelled against it, like Aleko in Pushkin's poem 'The Gipsies'. Art Belinsky now sees as an instrument by means of which the higher, intuitive reason – as opposed to ordinary reason or the mechanical, intellectual understanding – seeks to reveal truth. He believes that the artist should not moralize or act as a spokesman for ephemeral, local or factional interests, a failing for which Belinsky severely castigated Menzel, a minor German writer who had had the temerity to take Goethe to task for his detachment [20 *pp. 117–23*]. As for the creative process, Belinsky continues to see the artist as not entirely in control of his work; inspiration does not come when the artist wishes and as he wills it. The essays of this phase are published in *The Moscow Observer (Moskovskii nabliudatel')* and then, after the failure of this journal, in *Notes of the Fatherland (Otechestvennye zapiski*), published in St Petersburg, to which Belinsky moved late in 1839.

Thirdly, from the early 1840s Belinsky turns from German philosophy to French radical ideas and literature, argues that in certain times and places – including the Nicholaevan age in Russia – art is obliged to serve as a mirror to society, and expresses sympathy for the downtrodden.

Belinsky's sense of revulsion at his Hegelian self is most explicitly expressed in his personal correspondence, particularly in his voluminous letters to Botkin, where for example he curses his 'vile yearning to be reconciled with vile reality' and now sets 'the human personality higher than history, higher than society, higher than humanity' [20 *p. 124*]. Belinsky's rejection of Hegel is accompanied by expressions of compassion for the sufferings of his fellow man, by a fanatical interest in the teachings of French utopian socialists, and by a willingness, it seems, to contemplate revolutionary bloodshed with equanimity [20 *pp. 126–9*]. Belinsky's new mood is manifested in literary criticism too, especially in two articles on the rebellious young poet and prose writer Lermontov in which Belinsky for the first time revealed an admiration for the Romantic hero in conflict with his society. By 1842 Belinsky's more radical stance was finding expression in defence of the rights of women (and interest in the work of the French woman writer George Sand); in approval of the tendency of contemporary writers to address social questions in their work; in an interest in the novel as a genre capable of exploring complex social and personal relationships; and in attacks on Romanticism, which Belinsky now considers representative of an inner emotional and spiritual world divorced from the external world where real life, nature and history unfold. The modern age, he now contends, rejects art for its own sake: art cannot any longer confine itself to pleasing 'birdsong' which shuts out worldly sufferings. It is a viewpoint that colours the monumental cycle of eleven essays in which, over the years 1843–46, Belinsky reviewed the whole *oeuvre* of the poet Pushkin, who had been killed in a duel in 1837, and established Pushkin's seminal importance in Russian literature. The content of Pushkin's poetry Belinsky defined as tender, noble, refined, humane and morally educative, and its form he characterized as charming and graceful. And yet Belinsky feared that humaneness and tolerance might breed a resignation to current conditions of the sort he himself now abjured. Therefore Pushkin, for all his importance in Russian literature, seemed to Belinsky from the vantage point of the mid-1840s a poet of an outdated type in an analytical age, an elitist at a time when the mass could not be ignored.

Belinsky's concern in his later years to encourage the development of a realistic, socially engaged literature was accompanied by a search in works of art for what was of general, typical significance and therefore of sociological importance in them. He now accepted the role of reason, as well as poetic fantasy and inspiration, in the creative process. He demanded that humanistic values and sympathy for the poor be injected into art, and he encouraged a 'Natural School' of writers who upheld the rights of oppressed classes and of women and who censured apathy, ignorance and slavish adherence to custom. At the same time Belinsky led the Westernizers' attack on the Slavophiles, chiding or mocking the Slavophiles for their idealization of pre-Petrine Russia, their paternalistic pleas to their compatriots to show humility, their predictions of the impending ruin of the West, and their fondness for quaint native customs and costume. In common with the other Westernizers he also revered Peter the Great as the ruler who had laid foundations for the modernization and civilization of Russia.

The significance of Belinsky in the history of Russian literature, the process of the formation of the Russian intelligentsia and the development of opposition to autocracy is very great. His concern for the development of Russian literature as a whole, as opposed to the appearance of successful individual works, was reflected in the annual surveys of its condition which he wrote in each of the last eight years of his life. That he was able by 1848 to detect in Russian literature a coherence lacking when he made his debut in 1834 was in no small measure due to his own efforts and influence. He performed the essential tasks of discriminating among the plethora of works being published (and his judgements in the main continue to hold good), guiding a readership in its infancy and cultivating taste. Most importantly, he lent imaginative writing in Russia the status of a sacred vocation, a status famously described in the impassioned letter which in 1847 he wrote to Gogol from a Silesian spa to which his friends had sent him in the hope of arresting the deterioration in his health. This letter – an injured response to Gogol's apparent defence of the existing order in a work entitled *Selected Passages from Correspondence with Friends* [11] – could not be published in Belinsky's lifetime or in the years following his death, but it was widely known in manuscript form and was regarded as his testament [*Doc.* 7] [106; 110; 120; 121].

HERZEN

Comparable with Belinsky in standing as a thinker is Herzen, the illegitimate but acknowledged son of a wealthy Russian nobleman and a German girl. Of all the nineteenth-century Russian thinkers Herzen is perhaps the best known to a Western readership by virtue of the intellectual accomplishment and stylistic elegance of his writings (more of which have been translated into English than has work by other Russian thinkers of the period), his involvement in Western intellectual and political life during long years of emigration, the relative accessibility and congeniality of his thought to a liberal readership, and the reverence with which major post-war Western scholars, notably Isaiah Berlin [68 *pp. 186–209*], have regarded him. This familiarity may seem to confer on Herzen a precedence over other Russian thinkers which within the context of Russian thought itself is not warranted. Nevertheless his importance is undeniably great and manysided. As a representative of the more radical wing of the Westernism of the 1840s, and like the so-called Young Hegelians or Left Hegelians in Germany at this time, Herzen turned Hegel's philosophy to use as a tool for political opposition rather than conservatism. He contributed to the Russian prose fiction of the 1840s and in the 1860s produced memoirs of exceptional breadth, zest and literary quality [14]. Together with Bakunin (see pp. 70–72) he was Russia's first major dissident political émigré in modern times and a mordant critic of the bourgeois values which he encountered on emigration. In the late 1840s and early 1850s he popularized – though he alone did not invent – a vision of a distinctive national form of socialism that was to be taken up by Populists in the late 1860s and which underpinned revolutionary strategy for two decades. He served as publisher of a large uncensored literature printed abroad. He also aspired to the development of the personality emancipated from all absolutes and warned of the perils of surrender to any authority, religious, political or philosophical, or to revolutionary zeal.

The beginning of Herzen's struggle with autocracy dates from his teenage years. In 1826 – at least in Herzen's own, no doubt somewhat embroidered, version of events – he secretly vowed, as a fourteen-year-old boy, to avenge the Decembrists and in 1827 or 1828 he and his friend Ogariov took an emotional oath on Sparrow Hills outside Moscow to dedicate their lives to the struggle for liberty in Russia. In the years 1829–34, during and just after his career at Moscow University, a relative haven of free intellectual life in those years, Herzen, Ogariov and friends immersed themselves in German philosophy (notably Schelling) and the utopian socialism of Saint-Simon, absorbed through the writings of his disciples. Like Chaadaev they pondered questions relating to the philosophy of history and they searched for a system that would promise freedom and justice. However, in the post-Decembrist climate even such metaphysical pursuits brought about the arrest of Herzen, Ogariov and other members of their circle and resulted, for Herzen, in banishment, as a government clerk, to the remote provincial town of Viatka. (There followed a further two years of exile, from 1837 to 1840, in Vladimir, and then additional banishment, for an incautious remark in a letter to his father which was opened by the police, to Novgorod.) Herzen finally returned to Moscow in 1842 and began to participate vigorously in the intellectual life of the capital, currently animated by the debate between the Westernizers and Slavophiles. In his essays on *Dilettantism in Science* (1842–43) and his *Letters on the Study of Nature* (1845) – esoteric works still conceived within the Hegelian framework that so powerfully affected Russian thought in the late 1830s and early 1840s – he uses Hegel's dialectic as a tool to undermine existing orders rather than to support them, as Hegel himself had perhaps intended. The absolutes invented by religion and philosophy, Herzen believes, are relative to specific times and places. Only the authority of human reason is enduring. Moreover, through reason and its creation, science, people achieve not only inner liberation but also the capacity to change the world, once they correctly perceive it. Herzen comes therefore to an eighteenth-century view of reason as an instrument of progress [113 *ch. 10*]. In the same period Herzen wrote a novel, *Who is to blame?* (1845–46), which analyses character and society in the naturalistic manner demanded among the Westernizers and which includes in the character of Beltov – no doubt to some extent a thinly disguised portrait of Herzen himself – one of the classic depictions of the 'superfluous man' of the Nicholaevan period. The explanation of the weaknesses of the characters and of the restlessness of Beltov are to be found, it is implied, in Russian social and moral conditions [113 *ch. 11*].

As the rift within the Westernist camp developed, Herzen became somewhat distanced from the moderate faction. His growing interest in natural science and his attraction by Feuerbach's *Essence of Christianity* (1841) – in which the German Left Hegelian had set out to demonstrate that God was not a perfect being with an existence of His own but an ideal creation of human consciousness – led Herzen towards a philosophical materialism which Granovsky, for one, found unpalatable. Nor could the more liberal Westernizers approve Herzen's tendency now to idealize the Russian peasant, as the Slavophiles were doing, or his discovery of socialist potential in the peasant commune. Nor did they share his growing enthusiasm for the development of socialism that was taking place in France, where the humanistic interpretation of Christianity preached by Saint-Simon and Leroux was being supplanted by the more practical consideration of political opposition encouraged by Louis Blanc and Proudhon. These differences were soon to be exacerbated by a debate about the historical role of the bourgeoisie.

In 1846 Herzen's father died, bequeathing him a large fortune. Oppressed by Russian conditions and isolated from his few remaining friends, in January 1847 Herzen left Russia with his wife, three children and his mother, never to return. He settled first in Paris, perceived as the seat of European radicalism. Here he found a society which seemed to him in its own way no less moribund than Nicholaevan Russia (though as Martin Malia has shown, Herzen seems to have made up his mind even before leaving Russia that he would not find the Europe admired by the liberal Westernizers to his liking [113 *pp. 339–41*]). His disenchantment was eloquently expressed in his four 'Letters from the Avenue Marigny', which were published in *The Contemporary* in 1847. Whereas in Russia the government and a legion of bureaucrats spread gloom throughout the land, Herzen argued in these letters, in France it was the bourgeoisie that poisoned society with its ruthless exploitation and tawdry selfish values. Wealthy but parsimonious, ostentatiously patriotic, sentimental, hypocritical, and obsessed with profit, the bourgeoisie had devised a morality based on arithmetic, on the power of money and on love of order. To the more moderate Westernizers such as Granovsky and Botkin, Herzen's letters, with their view of the bourgeoisie as a class without a distinguished past and with no future, represented an unacceptably one-sided view and underestimated the positive contribution which the bourgeoisie had made to the development of Western civilization. Even Belinsky, who in 1846 had come round to acceptance of the need for a bourgeoisie in Russia, asserted in response that the bourgeoisie was a force for progress. Nevertheless it must be said that Herzen's letters set a tone for discussion of capitalist development in the Russian intelligentsia. It was the tone perhaps of the aristocrat who was no less hostile than the plebeian to the bourgeois, although he viewed the bourgeois from a different angle. This tone was to be a marked feature of Russian thought in the second half of the nineteenth century and one that was in the final analysis perhaps very damaging to Russia's economic and social development.

The failure of the revolutionary events in France in 1848 provided further disappointment to which Herzen gives vent in what is perhaps the cornerstone of his writings, *From the Other Shore*. This work is at one and the same time despairing and optimistic. In it Herzen indicts all attempts to build abstract rationalistic systems and abandons hope of inevitable progress but also recognises the individual as an end in itself and affirms the importance of the free personality as a creative force in the historical process. Herzen's unhappiness in this period was compounded by personal misfortunes. His mother and second son were drowned. His wife Natalie conducted an affair with the German poet Herwegh, memorably described by E. H. Carr [107 *ch.* 3–4], and indeed by Herzen himself, who in his memoirs strains to justify his own conduct in the episode. Then, in 1852, Natalie died.

Out of this despair, philosophical and personal, there emerges a view that Russia, thanks to the special qualities of her unspoilt peasantry, could play a leading role in Europe's social regeneration. Herzen's admiration for the common people had been developing for some time. It was apparent in the 'Letters from the Via del Corso' (1847–48), which together with the 'Letters from the Avenue Marigny' made up his *Letters from France and Italy* published as a single volume in the 1850s. (The 'Letters from the Via del Corso' are Herzen's first response to life in Italy and they reflect his enthusiasm for the independent spirit of the Italian cities and his corresponding antipathy to the centralized state [113 *p. 365*].) Now, in the period 1849–54, Herzen places an idealized view of the Russian peasant at the heart of the distinctive 'Russian socialism' which he expounds in a series of essays written in French and English and published abroad. Although Herzen had been among those who had recently berated the Slavophiles for their belief in Russia's national exclusiveness and superiority, he now claimed that in the Russian national life and character there lay the seeds of future greatness. To the Slavs in general he attributed intelligence, strength and adaptability, and on the Russian peasant he heaped especial praise. The Russian peasant, he argued, possessed an instinctive socialism which found expression in the commune, a miniature self-governing republic. In the commune the land belonged to all, not to individuals; each person had a right to the use of as much land as any other; each member who held land was entitled to a voice in discussion of the commune's affairs; and the officers of the commune were democratically elected at a general assembly. This age-old institution was held to have saved the Russian people from 'Mongol barbarism' and 'German bureaucracy' and now it might save them also from capitalism [*Doc. 9*]. Since there was no invariable predestination in history Russia might progress to socialism without passing through all the phases of Western European historical development [13 *pp. 165–208*; 105; 110; 113].

THE PETRASHEVTSY

Besides the conspicuous debates in the upper echelons of the intelligentsia between the Slavophiles and Westernizers and between the moderate Westernizers and radical Westernizers, fervid discussions of radical ideas, particularly French socialism, were also taking place in St Petersburg in the period 1845–49 at a more humble social level in numerous overlapping groupings of young men associated with an eccentric young nobleman, Butashevich-Petrashevsky. The Petrashevtsy, as those who frequented these circles were known, embraced at one time or another a wide array of talented young men: Danilevsky, a student of botany who in the late 1860s was to make an important contribution to the debate about Russia's relationship with the West with his book *Russia and Europe* [94]; the emergent writer Dostoevsky, whose first literary works, written in the spirit of the Natural School and warmly praised by Belinsky, had been published in 1846; Valerian Maikov, one of the earliest Russian exponents of positivism and at the age of twenty-three the leading literary critic of the journal *Notes of the Fatherland*; the civic poet Pleshcheev; and the satirist Saltykov. There was among the Petrashevtsy an element which planned to print illegal pamphlets and even dreamed of the formation of a conspiratorial organization and preparation of an insurrection, though how serious a threat they posed to the regime is problematical. This element was inspired by Speshnev, a charismatic exponent of the egoistic amoralism of the German anarchist Stirner and a model for the character of Stavrogin in Dostoevsky's *Devils*. Their circles detected by the police, many of the Petrashevtsy were arrested in April 1849 and in December that year twenty-one of them, including the young Dostoevsky, were marched on to Semionovsky Square in St Petersburg to be shot; at the last moment they were informed that their sentences had been commuted to various terms of hard labour and exile.

By virtue of both their social origin and their beliefs the Petrashevtsy prefigured developments in the intelligentsia after the Crimean War and in particular the thought of Chernyshevsky (see pp. 55–9), who in his student days himself frequented the periphery of this society. On the whole the Petrashevtsy represented a less elevated social stratum than the most prominent thinkers of the 1840s: they emanated from the ranks of the impoverished gentry and earned a living as petty clerks in government service which gave no outlet for their ambitious youthful idealism. They were attracted by materialism, atheism, utilitarian ethics, and the method of the natural sciences, and they believed in human perfectibility and the possibility of realizing a utopia. They avidly discussed the work of the early French socialist writers (Saint-Simon, Fourier, Louis Blanc, Pierre Leroux, Proudhon, Cabet, Considérant), who held sway in socialist circles in these days before the rise of Marxism and competing strands of German thought. They ruminated on the possible application of the ideas of these socialists in the stagnant reality of Nicholaevan Russia, like Herzen viewing the peasant commune as a basis for a future socialist order. Of the various utopian schemes put forward by the French writers, the one that held the greatest appeal for them was the so-called phalanstery (the word is a compound derived from 'phalanx' and 'monastery') of Fourier, a co-operative agricultural community of 1,800 people which Fourier supposed would take true account of the needs of human nature, satisfying human passions as he identified them, and remove the moral and social evils and economic wastefulness associated with capitalism. Fourier's views, and other socialist ideas, were propagated by Petrashevsky at social gatherings and by means of an ingenious device designed to evade the censors, compilation of a so-called *Pocket Dictionary of Foreign Words,* which included lengthy entries on such terms as 'nepotism', 'opposition', and 'Negrophile' (a term which gave scope for an attack on serfdom) [119; 132 *pp. 75–83*].

The activity of the Petrashevtsy was uncovered by the authorities in the wake of the intellectual ferment and uprisings of 1848–49 in France, Prussia, Austria, Hungary and other European countries. The discovery of the circles gave substance to the official fear that the revolutionary wave might engulf Russia too. This factor helps to explain the severity both of the sentences meted out to the Petrashevtsy and of the internal repression precipitated by the disturbances in the West. The 'dismal seven years' between 1848 and 1855 were harsh even by the standards of the reign of Nicholas and reminiscent of the period that had followed the Decembrist Revolt. Censorship was placed under the supervision of a secret committee chaired by the reactionary General Buturlin. Uvarov was replaced as Minister of Education by Prince Shirinsky-Shikhmatov, who saw himself as a blind instrument of the sovereign. Philosophy came to be regarded as a subversive subject and in universities the teaching of some branches of it was discontinued and the teaching of logic entrusted to theologians. The number of university students was reduced [45 *pp. 274–9*]. The relatively inoffensive Turgenev was banished to his country estate. In this atmosphere the intelligentsia, weakened in any case by the death of Belinsky and the emigration of Herzen, could not flourish, and the period is notable for the dearth of major contributions to thought and imaginative literature. The reaction ended only with the death of Nicholas, which marked a great divide in the history of opposition to autocracy and inaugurated a period of vigorous rebellion, to which we turn in the following chapter.

5 INTELLECTUAL REVOLT (1855–c. 1868)

THE EFFECTS AND AFTERMATH OF THE CRIMEAN WAR

The Crimean War arose ostensibly as a result of dispute with France over privileges for Catholics at the expense of the Orthodox in the Holy Places in Jerusalem, and over Russian ambitions to establish a protectorate over the Orthodox subjects of the Ottoman Empire. At a more fundamental level it reflected the concern of Western powers about a shift in the European balance of power in favour of an over-mighty, oppressive Russia. The outcome of the war – defeat on Russian territory at the hands of British and French forces operating at great distance from home, as well as Turkish forces – did not entail loss of territory, still less did it threaten Russia's status as a major European power or imperil the tsarist regime. Nevertheless the war does represent a watershed in Russian intellectual history and the history of opposition to autocracy. It punctured the sense of military invulnerability that had developed in Russia in the age of imperial expansion under Catherine and as a result of the heroic defence of the fatherland against Napoleon. It generated self-doubt and self-criticism. Most importantly it underlined the backwardness of Russia's economic and social structure and the urgency of the need for far-reaching change. Discussion of such change was facilitated by the sudden death of Nicholas after a minor illness in February 1855 and by the accession of his son, Alexander II, a man of milder temperament, to the throne. Convinced, as he famously warned the Muscovite nobility in 1856, that it was better to abolish serfdom from above than to wait until the serfs began to liberate themselves from below, Alexander initiated debate about emancipation and authorized preparation of legislation. The edict which he eventually approved on 19 February 1861 freed the serfs from their masters and provided for the allocation to them of plots of land, for which, however, they would have to pay 'redemption dues' over a protracted period. Extensive legal reform, consequential on the liberation of the majority of the population from the juridical power of the nobility, and various educational, economic and military reforms, were also implemented in the course of the 1860s. And yet public opinion was not reconciled with autocracy, not least because the emancipation failed to relieve the economic hardship of the majority of the rural population and because the government continued to resist the political reform that these changes seemed to require. Thus under Alexander II opposition to autocracy, far from abating, took more radical forms: in the late 1850s, as factions began to crystallize in the intelligentsia, a younger generation of thinkers undertook a comprehensive reappraisal of traditional values and from the early 1860s a revolutionary tide, fed by the Western socialist movement but taking a course of its own, began to swell.

In the freer atmosphere of the early years of Alexander's reign, cultural and intellectual life again began to flourish. Given the interdependence, during the reign of Nicholas, of imaginative literature, on the one hand, and aesthetic, ethical, social and political ideas, on the other, it is not surprising that the sudden revival of thought after the Crimean War should have been accompanied by the appearance of a profusion of important works of literature. These works included Tolstoy's *Sevastopol Stories* (1855–56); *Provincial Sketches* (1856–57), Saltykov's satirical depiction of official mores; Pisemsky's novel *A Thousand Souls* (1858) and his play *A Bitter Lot* (1859); Goncharov's novel *Oblomov* (1859), which through its eponymous central character identified the inertia thought to be symptomatic of the pampered Russian nobleman; Ostrovsky's play *The Thunderstorm* (1860); *Notes from the House of the Dead* (1860), Dostoevsky's semi-fictional account of his years in prison; and Turgenev's four major novels *Rudin* (1856), *A Nest of Gentry* (1859), *On the Eve* (1860) and *Fathers and Children* (1862) – in which he was felt to have depicted the changing physiognomy of the educated Russian nobleman in the period from about 1840 to 1860.

A further sign of the cultural and intellectual renaissance of the post-Crimean period was the reinvigoration of certain journals and the appearance of new ones. The journals began to reflect increasingly clear positions on the political spectrum. Thus Slavophilism found expression in *The Day* (*Den'*) and in the late 1850s and early 1860s a 'native soil conservatism' (*pochvennichestvo*; see pp. 48–50) akin to Slavophilism was purveyed by *The Muscovite* (*Moskvitianin*) and then by the successive journals *The Time* (*Vremia*) and *The Epoch*

(*Epokha*), of which Dostoevsky (by now back in St Petersburg) was *de facto* editor. *The Library for Reading* (*Biblioteka dlia chteniia*), under the editorship of Druzhinin (see pp. 51–2), offered a defence of art for its own sake that had liberal or even conservative political implications. *The Russian Herald* (*Russkii vestnik*) served as a mouthpiece for an emergent liberalism, albeit a liberalism of a peculiarly statist Russian hue. *Notes of the Fatherland* and in particular *The Contemporary* (*Sovremennik*), in the hands of Nekrasov and Panaev and under the *de facto* editorship of Chernyshevsky, became the main forum for radical thought during the decade after the Crimean War. In the early 1860s *The Russian Word* (*Russkoe slovo*) adopted an even more extreme radical viewpoint, loosely termed 'nihilism', which towards the end of the decade after the closure of *The Russian Word*, was taken up by *The Deed* (*Delo*) [54]. (The three broad streams of thought represented by these journals – conservative nationalism, liberalism, and radicalism respectively – are dealt with separately and in that order in the following sections of this chapter.) The sudden flowering of public opinion in Russia, reflected in the resurgence of imaginative literature and the revival and expansion of journalism, was also stimulated by Herzen, who in 1852 had moved to London and who in 1853, with the aid of Polish exiles, established a 'free Russian press' there. From this uncensored printing house Herzen launched a new periodical, *The Pole Star* (*Poliarnaia zvezda*), in 1855 and then, in 1857, together with his friend from childhood days, Ogariov, now also an émigré, the newspaper *The Bell* (*Kolokol*). With its exposure of abuses which could not be openly publicized inside Russia, *The Bell* was read with interest in official circles as well as by the intelligentsia.

The differences between romantic conservative and Westernist thinkers that had emerged in the 1840s persisted in the 1850s, when the leading Slavophiles Khomiakov, the Aksakov brothers and Samarin remained active, and in the early 1860s when native-soil conservatism was formulated by Dostoevsky, Grigorev and Strakhov. At the same time a further major fissure developed in the intelligentsia within the Westernist camp itself. On one side of this fissure stood the older, more moderate men who had come to maturity in the reign of Nicholas and who hoped Russia could regenerate itself through piecemeal reform. These 'men of the 40s', or the 'fathers' in the terminology of Turgenev's major novel, were advocates of evolution: gradual, peaceful change from above. On the other side stood the 'men of the 60s' as they came to be known, the 'sons' who had come to challenge the 'fathers' and whose outstanding fictional representative is Bazarov in Turgenev's masterpiece. These younger, more radical men were impatient for thoroughgoing transformation and in the last analysis looked with equanimity on the prospect of revolutionary upheaval. The two sides are characterized by the markedly different tones and demeanour that Turgenev has captured in his novel. The formality, civility and elegant manners and dress to which the older generation attach such importance are rejected by the younger generation as the hypocritical conventions of an obsolescent class; the young cultivate instead a freedom, casualness, even carelessness, of appearance and conduct. Beyond these superficialities lies a deeper divergence of values. The more moderate fathers, at least according to Turgenev's humane depiction of them, respect the individual human personality and cherish family relationships and friendship. The young, on the other hand, view the human individual as an organism that behaves in a predictable way according to natural laws which are discoverable by science, and they conceive of close human relationships as a product of mutual self-interest or ideological affinity. Their differences, in Turgenev's novel, are encapsulated in their contrasting attitudes to nature: whereas for the fathers the natural world represents a universe with which they empathize and its beauty is inextricably associated with their own innermost personal joys, for the apparently pragmatic nihilist Bazarov nature is not a temple but a workshop in which he can study with a view to ascertaining immutable laws that explain human, as well as animal, organisms. To some extent the two factions within the Westernist intelligentsia represented the standpoints of different classes as well as different generations. The 'men of the 40s' were on the whole members of the nobility, such as Annenkov, Druzhinin and Turgenev himself (although their companion Botkin emanated from the merchant class). Among the 'men of the 60s', on the other hand, we find more so-called *raznochintsy*, that is to say men of varied backgrounds but of lower social status than the gentry, for example representatives of the petty bourgeoisie (*meshchanstvo*) and the merchant class (*kupechestvo*), and members of the embryonic professional class such as doctors, who enjoyed relatively humble status in nineteenth-century Russia.

One social feature of the militant young faction of the intelligentsia which requires comment is the prominence among them of the sons of the lower clergy. Both Chernyshevsky and Dobroliubov, the two leaders of the radical intelligentsia in the five or six years after the Crimean War, belonged to this group. So too did Antonovich and Eliseev, two of the most militant publicists of the 1860s, Nikolai Uspensky, a writer of short, naturalistic sketches on peasant life, and

Pomialovsky, a powerful prose writer who was beginning to examine the spiritual character of the *raznochintsy* as a dislocated social stratum when he succumbed to alcoholism at the age of twenty-eight. Jocularly known as *popovichi*, these sons of the lower clergy experienced the same poverty as the majority of the rural population but perhaps because they were literate and had access to fiction and publicism sensed their hardship more keenly than most and sought means of escape more avidly. At the same time it is possible that their ecclesiastical background gave them a strong sense of the world as a struggle between principles of good and evil, and imparted a moral or religious colouring and a millenarian zeal to their thought even when they had abandoned Christian doctrine for materialism and atheism.

CONSERVATIVE NATIONALIST THOUGHT IN THE 1850s AND 1860s

The Slavophiles of the 1840s were weakened by several deaths among their number – the two Kireevsky brothers died in 1856, and Konstantin Aksakov and Khomiakov both died in 1860. Nevertheless Slavophilism, like other strands of thought, underwent a revival in the new conditions after the Crimean War. One manifestation of that revival was Konstantin Aksakov's memorandum to Alexander on the internal state of Russia, which was examined above (see pp. 28–9). Another was a so-called epistle to the Serbs written by Khomiakov and co-signed by other leading Slavophiles such as the Aksakov brothers, Kosheliov and Samarin. In this open letter to the people of Serbia, Khomiakov offered fraternal advice to fellow Slavs, lecturing them on the social importance of the Orthodox faith which they shared with the Russians and which alone offered clear understanding and sincere brotherhood, and eulogizing the supposed Orthodox willingness, expressed in the peasant commune, to submit unquestioningly to a collective will [*Doc. 11*]. Both Kosheliov and Samarin, moreover, were authors of thoughtful projects for the emancipation of the serfs.

However, nationalist thought also began to find expression in the related but distinct 'native-soil conservatism' that sprang up in the late 1850s and early 1860s and that, like Slavophilism, found itself ill-at-ease with the modern bureaucratic tsarist state. The native-soil conservatives (*pochvenniki*) – among whom the literary critic Grigorev, the future novelist Dostoevsky, and the critic Strakhov were the most prominent – re-examined the problem of Russia's national identity and joined the debate as to which alien institutions and values it was prudent to adopt and which native ones it was important to sustain. They pondered means of bridging the gulf that separated the educated class from the masses and they bemoaned the fate of the alienated intellectual at odds with his society, rootless and lacking inner equilibrium or moral certainty. Their fear of the encroachment of capitalism in Russia and their belief that people would become dehumanized in the modern industrial setting led them to defend a mainly agrarian communal society not dissimilar from that envisaged by some contemporary radicals (see pp. 57, 60) and the early Populist revolutionaries (see pp. 67, 69, 72). On the other hand their emphasis on the need to reconcile conflicting interests in order to bring about social harmony brought them closer to the liberals (even though they despised the liberals' constitutionalism and could not understand their respect for the temporal law) than to the radicals who shared their distaste for capitalism. While liberals such as Kavelin (see pp. 31, 52) sought to blur social distinctions by advocating equality before the law (though not the erosion of economic differences), the native-soil conservatives looked forward to a society in which the gentry, petty bourgeoisie, and peasant, united by the Russian's supposed innate sense of brotherhood, might co-operate with one another in the service of a large national purpose. Ironical as it might seem, this emphasis on reconciliation eventually led the native-soil conservatives into open conflict with the radical thinkers, who were not to be satisfied with half-measures. In any case the revolution envisaged by the native-soil conservatives was a moral one which would concern the inner life of the spirit rather than the external forms of social organization which radical thinkers regarded as the main sources of poverty, crime and misery [87; 88; 90].

To some extent 'native-soil conservatism' finds expression in the great novels – *Crime and Punishment*, *The Idiot*, *The Devils*, and *The Brothers Karamazov* – which Dostoevsky came to write once he had clarified his outlook in his journalistic contributions to this strand of thought in the early 1860s. Some of Dostoevsky's ideas perhaps owe something to Grigorev's 'organic criticism', which is grounded in a belief in the primacy of artistic creativity for mankind and in the inseparability of that creativity from distinctive national cultures and histories. For example Grigorev, as Dostoevsky was later to do, put forward a theory of Russian types, positing a humble type, which he associated with the Slavs, and a predatory type, which he associated with Russia's early Varangian rulers. He also attributed universality to the Russian character and conceived Pushkin as the supreme manifestation of that universality. In the draft of a travelogue on his stay in the West in 1857–58 Grigorev even prefigured the bilious view of Western peoples presented in Dostoevsky's own record of his travels in the West in 1862, *Winter Notes on Summer Impressions*, with its derisive attitude to the slogan of the French Revolution, *Liberté, Égalité, Fraternité*, and its view of the rationalist utopia as an anthill [88; 89 iii].

It must be emphasized that although in his later journalism his conservatism and nationalism are explicit and harsh, Dostoevsky the artist transcends partisanship and even-handedly presents a multi-faceted view of reality. Nevertheless his novels clearly reflect and transmute into a timeless and universally valid presentation of profound metaphysical, ethical, social and political problems some of the major assumptions, anxieties and hopes of Russian conservative nationalist thought in general and of native-soil conservatism in particular. Dostoevsky rejects the optimistic view of the progress of Western civilization put forward by the Victorian historian Buckle. He admires the humility and true Christian piety of the simple Russian people. He notes the fragmentation of contemporary society. He is alarmed by the loss of religious faith, which is under attack from science, rationalism and scepticism, and by the growth of materialism, egoism and individualism, forces supposedly invading Russia from the West. He anticipates the moral anarchy and political tyranny to which nihilism, if unchecked, might lead, and he yearns for spiritual regeneration, moral revolution and the reconciliation of antagonistic social forces [89; 96].

RUSSIAN LIBERALISM AFTER THE CRIMEAN WAR

The years immediately following the Crimean War may be seen as the heyday of liberalism in nineteenth-century Russia, if by 'liberalism' we understand advocacy of freedom of expression, abolition or relaxation of censorship, and implementation of reform by the government in an atmosphere of stability and security. These years were Russia's first age of *glasnost'* (the word was used at this time, to indicate a greater openness and transparency in public affairs and a broadening of the parameters of permissible debate). Liberals, perhaps for the only time in tsarist Russia, found themselves more or less in harmony with the autocracy. After all it was the autocrat himself who had stimulated discussion of the most fundamental social reform, abolition of serfdom. Their writings, including detailed projects for the emancipation and other proposals relating to social and administrative questions, could be published legally, although much literature of this sort also circulated in manuscript form inside Russia or was published in the nine anthologies printed by Herzen in London on his free press in the years 1856–60 under the title *Voices from Russia*. Liberal thinkers such as Kavelin and enlightened bureaucrats and government ministers such as N. A. Miliutin, who played an important role in the editorial commissions preparing the ground for the emancipation and who in 1858 was appointed Deputy Minister of the Interior, mixed freely. Liberals were filled with admiration for Alexander, praised him fulsomely and were overcome with gratitude to the 'tsar-liberator' when the decree emancipating the serfs was finally published.

The values of Russian liberals in the intelligentsia in the late 1850s found their clearest expression, odd as it may seem at first sight, in a polemic about art. Liberals sought to preserve nobility, understood in a spiritual as well as a social sense, and to uphold the values of objectivity and moderation by defending an art unconstrained by topical social and political demands. (This position was similar to that adopted by Belinsky in his Hegelian phase.) The main champion of uncommitted art was Druzhinin, who became editor of *The Library for Reading* late in 1856, and he was supported in this enterprise by Annenkov, Botkin and the novelist Turgenev. These men glorified the heritage of the poet Pushkin and exhorted modern Russian writers to establish a 'Pushkin school' of Russian literature. In the course of a protracted polemic with Chernyshevsky (see pp. 55–9) over the period 1855–58 apropos of the major works of Russian literature appearing in those years, Druzhinin denigrated 'didactic' art and reproached Belinsky for his role in promoting it and commended instead the Olympian detachment and serenity displayed, Druzhinin believed, by such poets as Homer, Shakespeare and Goethe. Whereas didacticism, Druzhinin argued, impoverished literature in various ways, dispassionate art had a lasting beneficial moral effect on society by awakening in readers an appreciation of 'poetry', broadly defined.

The appeal of this view of art beyond Druzhinin's own generation was limited by its conservative implications. 'Pushkinian' values, as Belinsky had argued in his cycle of essays on Pushkin as far back as the middle of the 1840s, were *passé* and socially innocuous. The liberal position therefore put no pressure on a government traditionally reluctant to reform. Objectivity could even be interpreted as indifference to the plight of the masses. Moreover, the cult of the serene poet and the advice that he should not come down to the level of the crowd, Shakespeare's 'vile multitude', smacked of an elitism that was no longer fashionable. Such conservatism even came out in Druzhinin's distinguished work as a translator of Shakespeare: he described Kent, in his introduction to his translation of *King Lear*, with fondness as the 'faithful servant, the ideal of the true loyal subject', and he also elected at this period to translate *Coriolanus*, in which the eponymous warrior and selfless patriot is finally driven by the fickle and insolent tribunes of the people to desert the Roman cause [103 *ch. 5*].

The cautiousness and essential conservatism of Russian liberals after the Crimean War is manifested not only in their aesthetic standpoint but also in their stout defence of the interests of the nobility, their reluctance to tamper with the principle of autocratic government in Russia and their dependency on the benevolence of the autocrat. These aspects of contemporary liberalism are apparent in a 'Memorandum on the Emancipation of the Peasants in Russia', one of the most important projects on the subject, which was written by Kavelin in 1855, and in a supplement to it written the following year. Although he advocated complete liberation of the serfs from dependence on the lords and apportionment of land to them, Kavelin was anxious to ensure that the reform would jeopardize neither the social standing nor the economic well-being of the nobility. He insisted that the lords be compensated, in full and in advance, for the loss of their serfs as well as their land, argued in favour of continuation of large-scale private landownership by the nobility and tried to ensure that the lords' landholdings would indeed remain substantial after the emancipation by proposing that the peasants receive only so much land as they currently cultivated. He was far from advocacy of a *laissez-faire* post-reform economy which might undermine the pre-eminent position of the landed nobility in favour of a bourgeoisie. As for autocracy, the Russian tsar is seen by Kavelin as a figure who towers over sectional interests, a mediator and arbitrator who impartially judges the claims of all classes, showing preference for none [100; 103 *ch. 6*].

The bulk of the liberals of this post-war period, as 'men of the 40s', nourished a rather misty idealism that is conveyed in a celebrated essay of Turgenev's, 'Hamlet and Don Quixote' (1860). In this essay Turgenev draws a schematic distinction, which owes much to German sources, between what he believes are diametrically opposite types of personality: on the one hand the Hamlets, believing in nothing outside themselves, racked by doubt and scepticism and unable to apply themselves to any useful activity, and on the other hand the Quixotes, admirable idealists who live for something outside themselves and are indeed able to dedicate their lives to active service in some noble cause. It was essentially quixotism that distinguished the liberals such as Granovsky and Kavelin from a man who is in many respects ideologically close to them, Chicherin, an important thinker who stands at the conservative end of the liberal spectrum [102]. Chicherin's credentials as a liberal opponent of autocracy in the years following the Crimean War are undeniable. He was a leading contributor to the manuscript literature which gave expression to an embryonic liberal opinion. He attacked the aristocracy and presented their continued privilege as incompatible with the needs of an ethical modern state which existed, he believed, to subordinate the demands of individuals and estates to a rational plan promoting the general welfare. He advocated abolition of serfdom and the granting of a set of individual rights, freedom of expression, conscience and the press, academic freedom, publicity of governmental activity and legal proceedings – which amounted to a minimum liberal political programme. Nor did his view of the importance of the state in Russian history or his belief in the continuing need for reform within the framework of a strong state set him apart from the liberals of the older generation. And yet the latter did not accept him as one of their own and Kavelin censured him for the spirit of his criticisms of Herzen. As *engagé* intellectuals the 'men of the 40s' did not prize Chicherin's notion of scholarly integrity and his exclusion of moral concern and emotion from his thought and they tended to find him abrasive, arrogant, formal, distant and cold.

For all his independence and integrity, his advocacy of academic values and civil rights, Chicherin increasingly gave succour in various ways to autocracy. For example, he commended the French system of government over the English because it maintained the centralized state which Chicherin considered a prerequisite for the full development of freedom. He appealed to students of Moscow University, in which he occupied a chair from 1861 to 1868, to obey the law of the state irrespective of its perceived moral legitimacy. His relations with the court became close in the early 1860s; he took a patriotic stance on the Polish Revolt of 1863; and he deplored the lack of a concept of limits in the Russian mentality and urged Russians to develop a sense of proportion and moderation. While declaring an enthusiasm, in a treatise *On Popular Representation* (1866), for the electoral principle and representative government he also argued that such government could only operate successfully given certain preconditions, such as a mature political society, that were plainly lacking in Russia and he even expressed a preference for 'honest autocracy' over 'bankrupt representation'. And yet such conservatism was unexceptional in the liberal camp after 1861, when opinion in the intelligentsia quickly polarized. Annenkov, Botkin, Druzhinin and Kavelin too all chose loyalty to the autocrat in the interests of political and social stability, fearing that a triumphant socialist opposition would by accident or design bring about uncontrollable destruction. This choice entailed a loss of influence in the intelligentsia, an outcome of which, in truth, these liberals had had presentiments as far back as 1856. Their predicament is poignantly conveyed in fiction by the retirement of Pavel Kirsanov, in Turgenev's *Fathers and Children*, to the aesthete's foreign haven of Dresden. (It was in Dresden too, incidentally, that Annenkov, who like Turgenev himself spent most of the last twenty years of his life abroad, was to die in 1887.)

It should be added, finally, that the émigré Herzen occupied political space somewhere between the liberals who have been examined in this section and the militant young thinkers who will be examined in the following section. In some respects he was closer in the years after the Crimean War to the liberal camp than to any other. Admittedly, he had not endorsed the liberal opinions expressed in the anthologies *Voices from Russia*; indeed he was himself criticized in the first of those anthologies by both Kavelin and, more intemperately, Chicherin for his impatience with autocracy and with a policy of cautious reform. Nevertheless he too placed high hopes on Alexander for a while. Thus in 1856, echoing the words of Julian the Apostate to Christ, he congratulated Alexander, who had just announced his intention to abolish serfdom: 'You have conquered, Oh Galilean!'. Herzen also reproached the radicals of *The Contemporary* for their derisive attitude towards the liberals who were striving honourably to civilize their society after the reign of Nicholas. He quarrelled with Chernyshevsky, who had met him on a visit to London in 1859 and who damningly described him to Dobroliubov as 'Kavelin squared' [103 *p. 190*]. And yet following the emancipation, which he considered a betrayal of the peasants, Herzen again lost faith in the state. He now called on the youth to go to the people, expressed support for the Polish Revolt of 1863, and in 1865 moved to Geneva in order to be closer to the growing and increasingly militant young Russian émigré community there. Not that his support for the revolutionary wing of the intelligentsia was ever unequivocal: in 1869, the year before his death, his old fears about the cost of revolution found renewed expression in the 'Letters to an Old Comrade' which he addressed to Bakunin.

RADICAL THOUGHT: CHERNYSHEVSKY

Of the radical thinkers who effected a revolution in Russian thought after the Crimean War, the first and most important was Chernyshevsky [109; 116; 117; 118; 122]. Born in 1828 in Saratov, on the bank of the Volga at the easternmost boundary of Europe, Chernyshevsky was educated first in a local seminary and then, in the 1840s, at St Petersburg University. A product, then, of the depths of provincial Russia and of Russia's 'window on to Europe', to use Pushkin's description of St Petersburg, Chernyshevsky displays at one and the same time both the frame of mind of an ascetic, ecclesiastical caste and the erudition and approach to rational knowledge of a secular and thoroughly Westernized thinker. His thought betrays both a messianic zeal and a willingness to surrender to schematic designs of the Germanic sort that so attracted Russian thinkers from Belinsky to Lenin. He exemplifies the tendency that is marked in Russian thought to strive for what may be called an 'integral *Weltanschauung*' (the awkwardness of the expression testifies to the foreignness of the concept within an English intellectual framework). That is to say he tries to construct a rigid system of belief coherent in all its parts which will provide both a comprehensive explanation of all phenomena and a guide to living.

Chernyshevsky was concerned to replace what he saw as *a priori* notions or even cherished prejudices – about the existence of God, the duality of spirit and matter, the coexistence of good and evil in human beings, the transcendent quality of beauty – with a demonstrably valid system of belief regulated by reason. Fundamental to his outlook – and to that of the radical critics of autocracy in general at this period – is a firm conviction in the efficacy of natural science as a force for good in the world and in the applicability of the method deployed by natural science to all human problems. For not only did the natural sciences such as medicine, physics, biology, chemistry – to which Chernyshevsky was fond of making allusions which now seem banal–promise to reduce suffering through disease and to increase prosperity through technological progress. They also enabled their practitioners – who proceeded empirically, observing, measuring, conducting experiments and testing conclusions – to formulate incontestable laws which held good in all circumstances. Natural science therefore seemed capable of providing comprehensive explanations of all phenomena. Moreover, the rubicon separating the world of facts (the territory of metaphysics) from that of values (the territory of ethics and political philosophy, with which Russian thinkers were now primarily concerned) was easily, almost imperceptibly, crossed. The natural sciences therefore came also to be regarded as an infallible key to social, economic and even psychological and moral problems.

Chernyshevsky launched his intellectual rebellion in 1855 in a dissertation for a master's degree at St Petersburg University on the apparently abstruse subject of the 'aesthetic relationship of art to reality'. The direct object of his attack was the work of the German aesthetician Vischer, but behind this object stood the aesthetic system of Hegel and beyond Hegel the Platonic notion that above the transient, concrete, everyday world there lies a higher world of ideal forms whose beauty may be captured by the artist. To Chernyshevsky this dualistic aesthetic system, with its juxtaposition of an imperfect here-and-now and a transcendent world that we may briefly glimpse but never securely attain, encourages a tragic view of human life and stoical resignation to one's fate. In order to combat the political quiescence encouraged by such attitudes, Chernyshevsky redefines the beautiful as that which reminds us most vividly of life itself. Our aesthetic ideal, he contends, is that which is vital and vigorous. Moreover conceptions of beauty, he argues, are relative; what is considered vital varies depending on the class of the subject. Having reduced reality to one plane and redefined beauty accordingly, Chernyshevsky also limits the jurisdiction of the artist: his function is to reproduce reality, as the author of a handbook might, with a view to showing people what they have not seen or understood before [20 *pp. 199–202*].

In the years 1855–56 Chernyshevsky produced a long cycle of essays on what he termed the 'Gogol Period of Russian Literature' in which he implicitly laid claim to the mantle of Belinsky, or at least to the mantle of the Belinsky of the early 1840s who had championed a committed literature. Thus while the liberal Westernizers were defending the Olympian detachment of Pushkin Chernyshevsky advocated the artistic engagement and social criticism with which Gogol and Belinsky were felt to be associated. The critic approaching literature in this way would exploit the appearance of a new work of art as an occasion for commentary on the social conditions or factors that had given rise to it. The approach is exemplified in essays by Chernyshevsky himself on Nikolai Uspensky's sketches of peasant life, in which Chernyshevsky addresses the question as to the likeliness of peasant revolt, and on Turgenev's short story 'Asia', in which the critic uses the highly poetic, nostalgic recollection by Turgenev's narrator of an unfulfilled affair as a pretext for an exposé of the fecklessness of the serf-owning Russian gentry.

However, relatively little of Chernyshevsky's attention after 1855–56 was devoted to aesthetic or literary matters, partly no doubt because he was confident that these would be capably handled by the like-minded Dobroliubov, who began writing regularly for *The Contemporary* in 1857, and partly because the parameters of debate widened so quickly after the Crimean War that it became possible to venture into more overtly social, economic and political fields. It is indicative of the clarity of the socialist vision of the younger generation that by 1858 Chernyshevsky was taking up Herzen's defence of the peasant commune as an embryonic socialist institution. While he saw the commune as a feature of the existence of all peoples at a primitive stage of their development rather than as a precious institution exclusive to the Slavs, he did believe, like Herzen, that it might serve as an antidote to the Western ill of proletarian misery. In an article entitled, with characteristic inelegance, 'A Critique of Philosophical Prejudices against Communal Landholding', Chernyshevsky argued that backward societies did not invariably have to repeat all the stages of development undergone by more advanced ones and that Russia might proceed directly from its current semi-feudal condition to a form of socialism based on the peasant commune without passing through a protracted phase of capitalist development [20 *pp. 207–12*]. In other articles of the same period – the period, it should be remembered, when the emancipation of the serfs was being considered – Chernyshevsky stressed the economic as well as the moral virtues of communal landholding, taking issue with those who saw the commune as an inefficient, unproductive agricultural unit.

The growing confidence of the young socialists is reflected in Chernyshevsky's attacks, written in the same period as his articles in defence of the peasant commune, on his 'liberal' opponents in the intelligentsia who argued for gradual social change. In a number of essays on the apparently remote subject of French political history he fosters a view of Russian liberals as indecisive, unpractical, prone to high-sounding but essentially vacuous utterances and hypocritical in their defence of various rights and freedoms. 'Liberals', Chernyshevsky argued in an essay on 'The Struggle of Parties in France in the Reign of Louis XVIII and Charles X', set free speech and a constitutional structure above the material well-being of the masses. They did not understand that a legal right had value only when a person had the material wherewithal to take advantage of it. Unlike 'democrats', who were hostile to aristocracy and hoped to break the traditional domination of the upper classes over the lower in society, 'liberals' cherished a certain degree of 'aristocratism' and would not allow the balance of social power to be tipped in favour of the uneducated mass [*Doc. 12*] [20 *pp. 203–6*]. In a further article, on the eighteenth-century French physiocrat Turgot, Chernyshevsky obliquely expressed a fear that the ascendancy of liberalism in Russia would lead to the growth of a *laissez-faire* economy based on the principle of self-interest and would thus result in even greater hardship than the system it replaced.

The redefinition of values on which Chernyshevsky had embarked in his dissertation on aesthetics is completed in an essay of 1860 entitled 'The Anthropological Principle in Philosophy', which is notable for its further application of the reductionism that had eliminated a transcendent plane in aesthetics. Following German thinkers such as Vogt (notorious for his assertion that the brain secretes thought just as the liver secretes bile), Moleschott (who had argued that mental processes should be seen purely as the product of physical stimuli), and Büchner (who explained consciousness as a physical state of the brain brought about by the movement of matter), Chernyshevsky attempts in this essay to popularize a crude materialism and determinism. He denies the existence of a spiritual aspect in man. He then asserts that thought is the product not of intuition or innate impulse but of sensation and external stimuli. The human will he belittles by redefining it as merely 'wanting', a phenomenon in a whole chain of cause and effect in which external factors play the main role. Character, and what we perceive as human goodness or badness, Chernyshevsky treats as moulded by environment. Consequently crimes – or 'bad actions', as Chernyshevsky prefers to call them – are explained after the manner of Robert Owen as the product of poverty.

Equally far-reaching and influential was the reductionist utilitarian ethical doctrine put forward in 'The Anthropological Principle in Philosophy'. Whereas it was conventional to attribute altruistic as well as selfish impulses to people, Chernyshevsky holds that human actions are invariably governed by self-interest. However, since humans are rational creatures they are also amenable to persuasion that their own best interest lies in the last analysis in co-operation with their fellows. According to Chernyshevsky's doctrine of 'rational egoism', humans must therefore be taught to derive their selfish pleasure from performance of actions which are of benefit to others. Judgement of actions as good or bad is to be made on the basis not of some absolute moral imperative but a relativistic criterion: an act is good or bad according to its consequences. It is good if it is useful, and the greatest good is that which is useful to the greatest number. In this hierarchy of interests – formulated, it should again be remembered, in the years in which the abolition of serfdom was being discussed – the 'interests of a large class stand higher than the interests of a small one'. Chernyshevsky's ethic has a mathematical exactitude which is pleasing to him (it represents the application of geometrical axioms such as 'the whole is greater than the part' to social problems) and is consistent with a socialism in which individual liberty is less important than collective welfare [*Doc. 13*] [*20 pp. 213–22*].

The outlook painstakingly – and often tediously – expounded by Chernyshevsky in his publicism between 1855 and 1862, when he was arrested for alleged complicity in the activity of revolutionary groups that were beginning to appear, eventually found fictional expression in his celebrated and highly influential novel *What is to be done?* [7]. The novel was written in prison, smuggled out, lost, recovered and published in *The Contemporary* in 1863. Here the socialist vision is clarified through Chernyshevsky's portraits of the 'new people', his heroes Lopukhov and Kirsanov – both, it should be noted, students of medicine and therefore devotees of the natural sciences – and his heroine Vera Pavlovna. These characters live in harmony, personal and social, according to the principles of rational egoism. Escaping from the oppressive institution of the family, the basic unit of existing social organization, Vera Pavlovna establishes a model for the socialist future in the form of an efficient co-operative of seamstresses. In one of a cycle of dreams in the novel she beholds a communistic utopia inspired by the Fourierist phalanstery and housed in a building reminiscent of that monument to nineteenth-century technological progress, the Crystal Palace. Above all these new people towers the figure of Rakhmetov, the 'flower of the best people', the 'salt of the salt of the earth', a proto-revolutionary who is preparing himself physically and mentally for future exploits and who – in an apparent abnegation of the determinism preached in 'The Anthropological Principle in Philosophy' – tempers his will by self-denial and by lying like a fakir on a bed of nails [116].

RADICAL THOUGHT: DOBROLIUBOV, PISAREV AND THE ARTS

Chernyshevsky, in his reappraisal of existing values, was closely supported by Dobroliubov, chief literary critic for *The Contemporary* from 1857 until his death from tuberculosis in 1861 at the age of twenty-five. Dobroliubov exemplified the tendency in Russian thought to use literary criticism for social and political ends. His purpose was not, as he frankly explained, to discuss the artistic qualities of the works he reviewed but to examine the social, moral and ultimately political questions which they raised. Thus his famous article

'What is *oblomovshchina*?', a review of Goncharov's *Oblomov*, was written not so much about the novel but rather apropos of it as a discourse on the degeneration of the 'superfluous man' in the conditions of post-Nicholaevan Russia [*Doc. 14*] [*9 pp. 174–217*; *20 pp. 228–34*]. Dobroliubov was primarily interested not in idiosyncratic literary characters, still less in lyrical descriptions of nature written for the sake of art alone, like those produced at this period by the poet Fet, but in the social type as depicted in realistic prose fiction. For types, as portrayed by a writer with insight, truthfully revealed processes taking place in society. Dobroliubov looked forward to the day when the 'superfluous man' would be replaced by the so-called 'positive hero', a man of more resolve who could be relied upon to take decisive action. However, within Dobroliubov's own lifetime it was slightly premature to expect the disoriented Russian *raznochinets*, socially displaced and as yet diffident, to take on that role. Thus as Dobroliubov noted in his essay 'When will the Real Day come?', in which he reviewed Turgenev's novel *On the Eve* (and in which he characteristically blurred the boundary between art and reality), it was in the person of a Bulgarian patriot, Insarov, that Turgenev had portrayed the man of action; the principal Russian males in the novel continue to display a lack of will and energy [*9 pp. 388–438*]. The common people, on the other hand, offered somewhat more hope to the socialist camp: in various essays on works depicting the lower social strata Dobroliubov endorsed Herzen's view of the peasants as the authentic Russian people and described them as serious-minded, practical, endowed with a moral purity lacking in the idle nobility and fit to play the part of free citizens after the impending emancipation [*9; 22; 109; 114; 121*].

The rebellion initiated by Chernyshevsky and Dobroliubov was taken to new extremes after the arrest of the former and the death of the latter, notably by Pisarev who though imprisoned from 1862–66 exercised a profound influence on radical thought up until his death from drowning at the age of twenty-seven in 1868. In several respects Pisarev shared Chernyshevsky's and Dobroliubov's convictions. Like them he rejected art for art's sake and demanded the application of the criterion of utility in judgements of works of art. He extolled natural science and prided himself on the rejection of all prejudices and superstitions, that is to say assumptions that could not be upheld by reason and empirical method. He preached a thoroughgoing materialism, endorsed Chernyshevsky's theory of rational egoism and wrote a favourable review, entitled 'The Thinking Proletariat', of Chernyshevsky's novel *What is to be done?* [*23 pp. 624–75*]. And yet Pisarev pressed Chernyshevsky's and Dobroliubov's ideas further than they pressed them or perhaps dared to press them. Unlike them, he wrote of the 'destruction of aesthetics' and unashamedly spoke of a good pair of boots as more useful than a play by Shakespeare. Most importantly he seems to have glimpsed, as is clear from one of two admiring essays he wrote on Turgenev's character Bazarov, the destructive potential of the individual who acknowledges only the authority of his own senses and who, liberated from external moral constraint, roams at large beyond conventional conceptions of good and evil. Depending purely on taste, such a figure, Pisarev accepted, might prove either a great benefactor of mankind or a monstrous criminal [20 *pp. 240–3*; 109; 114; 121].

The term 'nihilist' (*nigilist*), which gained currency as a result of its use in Turgenev's novel *Fathers and Children* and became a widespread label for all representatives of the radical youth in the 1860s, may seem something of a misnomer to us, at least when applied to Pisarev, nihilism's leading spokesman. For the radicals of the late 1850s and the 1860s, far from believing in literally nothing, placed great faith in science as a key to the world and a panacea for its problems. And yet destruction was indeed the essential first stage of their mission to remake the world: they wished first, as Turgenev's Bazarov again felicitously put it, 'to clear the ground'. 'Nihilism' therefore remains a convenient term with which to describe the outcome of the intellectual rebellion that had begun towards the end of the Crimean War with Chernyshevsky's ponderous dissertation on aesthetics and which culminated a decade later with an iconoclasm that shocked more moderate opponents of the regime, as well as the regime's supporters, and lent impetus to the revolutionary movement.

It should be added, finally, that the leaders of the intellectual revolt of the late 1850s and the 1860s not only used the arts as material for their publicism but also in turn had a profound effect on imaginative literature, painting and music. Writers, painters and musicians all heeded the demands of Chernyshevsky, Dobroliubov, Pisarev and their supporters for topical subject matter, 'denunciatory' treatment of established institutions and privileged classes, sympathetic attention to the plight of the masses and a realistic artistic manner. Thus many writers – for example Levitov, Reshetnikov, Sleptsov and Nikolai Uspensky – now offered naturalistic sketches of peasant life, descriptions of the hardship of the nascent proletariat, and portrayals of 'positive' heroes and heroines unencumbered by the values of the nobility and capable of translating convictions into action. There also appeared a school of artists, including Kramskoi, Miasoedov, Perov,

Repin, Surikov and Vereshchagin, who rejected the seemingly artificial classicism promoted by the Russian Academy, with its fondness for alien or mythological subject-matter, in favour of a more literal art depicting subjects of national and topical relevance. These painters came to be known as the *peredvizhniki* (or 'Wanderers' as they are sometimes called in English) on account of their practice of moving exhibitions of their painting from place to place with a view to taking their art beyond the galleries frequented by the wealthy urban classes and making it more widely accessible. They too looked on art as a vehicle for expressing civic ideals and dwelt on social injustice and inequality, as well as painting simple Russian landscapes and scenes from Russian history. In music a similar function was performed by a group of composers known as 'The Five' or the 'mighty handful' (*moguchaia kuchka*) and comprising Balakirev, Borodin, Cui, Mussorgsky and Rimsky-Korsakov. Building on foundations laid by Glinka and Dargomyzhsky, and guided by the critic Stasov, an enthusiastic interpreter of the ideas of Chernyshevsky, these composers rebelled against the seeming artificiality of the Italianate opera popular in the first half of the nineteenth century, insisted on the use of music to tell a story, freely introduced folk songs and motifs into their works and – most notably in Mussorgsky's *Boris Godunov* – treated the Russian peasant mass as a mighty historical force.

SEDITIOUS LITERATURE AND REVOLUTIONARY GROUPS IN THE 1860s

The radical intelligentsia had conducted itself with some caution while the abolition of serfdom was being prepared. However, once the emancipation edict was promulgated in February 1861 the radical wing of the intelligentsia was dismayed by what seemed the inadequacy of the measure and quickly became more belligerent. The new mood found expression in a spate of subversive leaflets. The authors of the first such leaflet, entitled 'The Great Russian', copies of which were scattered in St Petersburg and Moscow in July 1861, appealed to the educated classes to relieve the incompetent government of its power. A second issue of the leaflet, which was distributed in September 1861, contained a demand for a better solution to the peasant question, the liberation of Poland and a constitution. A third issue of the leaflet, which appeared later in the same month, predicted that popular rebellion would break out in 1863 if the demands previously made were not met. In a more militant proclamation, addressed 'To the Young Generation' by Mikhailov and Shelgunov and printed on

Herzen's press in London, the young were urged to explain the evils of the tsarist order to the people and the troops and the prospect of revolutionary violence was countenanced with equanimity. Copies of a further and still more bellicose proclamation, entitled 'Young Russia' and written in prison by a former student, Zaichnevsky, were scattered in St Petersburg and Moscow in May 1862. Zaichnevsky criticized Herzen for expressing the naive hope that socialism might be introduced by peaceful means in Russia, predicted a 'bloody and implacable' revolution which would demolish the 'foundations of contemporary society' and summoned the youth to take up their axes and 'beat the imperial party without pity' [*Doc. 15*].

The period following the emancipation was also marked by student disturbances which broke out in St Petersburg in September 1861 in protest against the plans of the new Minister of Education – Putiatin, a former admiral – for a stricter regime in the institution. In the spring of 1862 tension was further heightened by a series of fires which badly damaged certain quarters of St Petersburg. The cause of the fires was not reliably established but conservatives fanned the widespread suspicion that radicals had started them. Taken together the seditious leaflets, student unrest and suspected arson caused public alarm and began to weaken enthusiasm for reform. The beginning of the end of the period of freedom that had followed the Crimean War was marked by the arrest in 1862 of numerous people suspected of political offences, including Chernyshevsky, and by the brutal suppression of the Polish Revolt in 1863.

It was in this climate that the first revolutionary circles began to appear. In 1861–62 Serno-Solovevich led a group calling itself Land and Liberty which set up a lending library of illegal literature in St Petersburg and issued a paper [129 *ch. 10*]. In 1865 Ishutin, a Moscow student, founded a group named The Organization, which dreamed of an insurrection and established a link with a group in St Petersburg led by Khudiakov. From the periphery of Ishutin's organization, perhaps from a section of it melodramatically named 'Hell', a student Karakozov came forward in 1866 to attempt to assassinate Alexander. (The attempt was unsuccessful and Karakozov was duly hanged [129 *ch. 14*].) The enthusiasm of the government for reform declined. *The Contemporary* was closed in 1866. The mood among the young in the country's higher educational institutions became more fevered; many began to look forward to a peasant uprising or other apocalyptic event in the near future.

In the academic year 1868-69 disorders again broke out in the higher educational institutions of St Petersburg and Moscow. The unrest was now harnessed by Nechaev, a beguiling young artisan from the provincial textile-manufacturing town of Ivanovo. Nechaev succeeded in organizing a number of circles in St Petersburg before disappearing in March 1869 and fleeing to Geneva, where he won the confidence of the gullible Bakunin and of Ogariov, now enfeebled by infirmity and alcohol. Together with these émigrés Nechaev generated a further torrent of proclamations, written in a vengeful spirit and millenarian tone, hundreds of copies of which were posted to Russia from abroad during the spring and summer of 1869. In August that year Nechaev returned to Russia, armed with a melodramatic document signed by Bakunin and bearing the seal of a 'European Revolutionary Alliance', of which Nechaev was supposed to be a member, and in Moscow he again set about organizing student circles, now under the banner of a 'Committee of the People's Revenge' [128].

Nechaev's subsequent notoriety stems mainly from two sources: firstly, a document known as 'The Catechism of a Revolutionary', which he probably wrote in Switzerland together with Bakunin in the summer of 1869, and, secondly, a murder which he orchestrated and helped to carry out in November that year. The 'Catechism' is infamous for its espousal of the Machiavellian principle that the end justifies the means. In particular the 'Catechism' made it clear that the goal of revolution in Russia was of such overriding importance that any tactic that might promote it, including deception, extortion, blackmail, theft and even murder, would be legitimate. From the pages of the 'Catechism', which was read out at the trial of Nechaev's co-conspirators, the so-called Nechaevtsy, in July 1871, there emerged a picture of the revolutionary as a ruthless, self-abnegating figure who placed no value on human life, viewed all fellow humans as instruments to be used in the execution of the revolutionary master-plan, and whose personal wants and feelings have been wholly subordinated to the exigencies of the revolutionary struggle [*Doc. 16*]. The ruthlessness advocated in the 'Catechism' Nechaev himself put into practice in the murder of the student Ivanov, who was evidently less pliable than the other members of Nechaev's cell and whom Nechaev accused of planning to betray his organization. Ivanov was lured to a grotto in the grounds of the Agricultural Academy in Moscow and there he was pinned down by other members of the group while Nechaev beat and strangled him and finally shot him in the head. His body, weighted with bricks, was thrown through a hole which Nechaev had made in the ice on a nearby pond [128; 129 *ch.* 15].

Ivanov's body was discovered a few days after his murder and arrests and confessions shortly followed. Nechaev himself again fled the country but was arrested in Switzerland and extradited to Russia in 1872, tried in January 1873 and incarcerated in the Peter and Paul Fortress in St Petersburg, where he died in 1882. The Nechaevan episode in the Russian revolutionary movement, to which the trials of the Nechaevtsy and of Nechaev himself gave widespread publicity, understandably caused alarm in official circles and agitated public opinion. For Dostoevsky – whose novel *The Devils*, with its moral and social chaos and its apocalyptic imagery, grows out of precisely these historical events and the intellectual revolt and rifts in the intelligentsia that had preceded them – Nechaev seemed indicative of the nation's catastrophic loss of bearings. However, it is equally important, when considering the history of opposition to autocracy, to note that the *nechaevshchina* also caused revulsion within the socialist camp itself and marked the end, for the time being at least, of a cynical, manipulative and authoritarian attitude to revolutionary activity. The revolutionary activists of the 1870s were to be influenced by leaders of altogether different moral complexion and political persuasion, some of whose most influential works were appearing in precisely those years, 1868–69, in which Nechaev himself was active.

6 THE REVOLUTIONARY MOVEMENT IN THE 1870s

RADICAL LITERATURE AND THOUGHT, 1868-73

The years from about 1868-1873, like those following the Crimean War, represented another period of heightened intellectual and cultural activity in Russia. However, whereas in the earlier period revolt had taken the form mainly of rejection of old values, now a powerful, or seemingly powerful, revolutionary movement began to develop.

Two strands apparent in the late 1850s and early 1860s – firstly, interest in the popular masses and, secondly, interest in the development of the active new representative of the intelligentsia – again combined, following the intellectual iconoclasm of the 1860s, to prepare the ground for this movement. Mordovtsev surveyed the great peasant rebellions of Russian history (1870-71) and the ethnographer Maksimov produced popular sketches of peasant life (1871). The revolutionary hero depicted in Chernyshevsky's *What is to be done?* [7] is reincarnated, in a sense, in Sokolov's popular work *Renegades* (1866, republished 1872) in which the Stoics, early Christians, sectarians, utopians and socialists are all presented as beings of superior moral calibre who have chosen to live outside the imperfect societies into which they have been born. He or she reappears, often as a pilgrim to or propagandist among the people, in a further spate of works – Bazhin's *History of an Association* (1869), Mordovtsev's *Signs of the Times* (1869), Omulevsky's *Step by Step* (1870) and Kushchevsky's *Nikolai Negorev, or a Successful Russian* (1871) – published in those years when interest in the masses was reaching a new height. In place of the now defunct *Contemporary* the journal *Notes of the Fatherland*, taken over by Nekrasov, Saltykov and Mikhailovsky, began to serve as the main mouthpiece for the radical intelligentsia. A number of thinkers now came forward to weave various threads – beliefs long since articulated about the Russian peasant and the peasant commune; a keenly felt need for distinctive national identity; the thirst for positive action and self-sacrifice; distaste for capitalism – into a more or less coherent, if fanciful, revolutionary strategy which for the sake of convenience we shall label Populism.

The least known of these thinkers but arguably the one who best captured the spirit of the time was Bervi, who wrote under the pseudonym Flerovsky. Bervi was an eccentric, ascetic man of Scottish ancestry who, it seems, represented to Tolstoy a rather uncomfortable example of the 'simplified' intellectual that Tolstoy himself aspired to be. He spent much of his life in voluntary or enforced wanderings around Russia and on the basis of this experience and of his researches wrote an influential work entitled *The Condition of the Working Class in Russia* (1869) which belongs to the same loose genre of travelogue as Radishchev's *Journey from St Petersburg to Moscow*. Adducing copious visual and documentary evidence from his odyssey from the frozen tundra of the north to the arid deserts of the south, from the endless Siberian taiga to Russia's agricultural heartlands and inchoate industrial centres, Bervi set out to demonstrate, *pace* Engels (against whose *Condition of the Working Class in England* he implicitly pitches his own work), that the existence of the Russian masses is uniquely wretched. At bottom *The Condition of the Working Class in Russia* is an expression of moral outrage at the plight of the peasants and workers in the immediate post-reform period, but like Radishchev's earlier work it combines indignation with fashionable rational argument. For Bervi is a precise observer of the way of life of the people (a fact which makes his book a useful historical source) and he deploys the then developing tool of statistical analysis, which imparts a scientific quality to his work. Bervi helped to fix in the consciousness of the revolutionary youth respect and an almost religious compassion for the suffering Russian masses. He also re-articulated the beliefs, expressed two decades earlier by Herzen and fundamental to Russian Populism, that the Russian people were peculiarly socialistic in nature, that their commune represented an embryonic socialist institution, and that Russia was not bound to follow the same path of economic and social development as that taken by the West but might come to socialism by a different route. The popularity of Bervi's cocktail of outrage and compassion, documentary evidence and Rousseauesque nationalism is attested by the frequent reference to it both by the police, who uncovered many copies of it in caches of reading matter used by revolutionary groups, and by revolutionaries themselves who in their memoirs recalled its influence on them [20 *pp. 253–8*; 115].

Besides cultivating sympathy for the common people and repeating the views on national distinctiveness on which revolutionary strategy in the 1870s was to rest, radical thinkers of the late 1860s were compelled also to challenge the deterministic position, or 'fatalism' as Lavrov had called it, that Chernyshevsky had adopted, at least in 'The Anthropological Principle in Philosophy'. This they needed to do in order to give the aspiring revolutionary a theoretical basis for freedom of action. This task was addressed by Mikhailovsky, in his long essay 'What is Progress?' (1869). Mikhailovsky argued that the objective point of view obligatory in the natural sciences was inappropriate in sociology in which humans were the subject of study as well as the students. Sociologists could only arrive at the truth, Mikhailovsky contended, if they put themselves in the position of the sentient beings they were examining, thinking their thoughts and suffering their sufferings. While not wishing altogether to abolish the objective method, then, Mikhailovsky did demand that the subjective method serve as a 'higher control' [123].

LAVROV

A similar function to that of Mikhailovsky's essay 'What is Progress?' was performed by the single most important work of this period, from the point of view of the emergent generation of revolutionaries, Lavrov's *Historical Letters*, which were published in serial form in 1868–69 and appeared in a separate volume in 1870 [19]. In fact the *Historical Letters* restate views put by Lavrov in less accessible works written in the late 1850s and early 1860s about the need for ideals and the obligation to put them into practice. Having sought to establish in his first two letters that history was no less important a field of enquiry than the natural sciences and that a subjective method was inevitable and legitimate in it, Lavrov made a celebrated appeal to the intelligentsia, in his fourth letter, to pursue the ideal of social justice. Playing on the ambiguity of the Russian word *dolg*, which has the sense of both 'debt' and 'duty', Lavrov argued here that the members of the intelligentsia had incurred an enormous debt to the toiling mass of mankind for the privileged conditions that had enabled them to formulate their ideals. This debt Lavrov translated into a duty incumbent on the 'critically thinking minority' to renounce their privilege by putting the socialist ideal into practice [*Doc. 17*] [*20 pp. 261–8*]. No excuses for inaction would be tolerated: neither scholarly work divorced from society's pressing needs nor any fears about the possible futility of heroic deeds by solitary individuals would relieve the critically thinking minority of this obligation. Thus the *Historical Letters* place Lavrov in the tradition of the 'repentant nobleman' who, like

Radishchev eighty years before, had pleaded with his fellows to go with humility to the peasant hut in search of reconciliation and personal salvation.

Lavrov shortly attempted to give substance to his plea that ideals be translated into action by outlining a revolutionary strategy and taking practical steps to assist its implementation. In 1870 he escaped, with the assistance of a young revolutionary sympathizer named Lopatin, from internal exile in the then remote provincial town of Vologda and travelled to Switzerland, where many Russian students were congregating and where he assumed the role of one of the émigré leaders of the developing revolutionary movement. In the pages of a journal *Forward!* (*Vperiod!*) which he edited first in Zurich and then in London in the period 1873–77, Lavrov urged the idealistic youth to go to the peasantry – for it was not from the towns but from the villages that the Russian revolution would come – and to inculcate in them the socialist consciousness of which the educated minority had become aware. In common with most revolutionaries of this period Lavrov believed that the Russian peasant possessed the energy and purity needed for this task, that the indigenous practice of communal landholding provided the ground on which socialism might be built in Russia, and that the village assembly, or *mir*, might become the basic political element of the society of the future. When this goal had been achieved the revolutionaries would retire into the background, for the peasants themselves, once converted to socialism, would, it was fondly hoped, implement the necessary changes from below. Indeed it seemed to Lavrov essential that the revolution's prospective beneficiaries, the people, carry out the reconstruction of society themselves: wherever 'consciousness' had been imposed on the masses by an alien minority a new breed of exploiters had come to power over the bodies of those who had built the barricades [*Doc. 18*].

It should be emphasized that such a revolution was conceived by Lavrov – as by Bakunin and the majority of Russian revolutionaries in the 1870s – as economic and social rather than political. That is to say Lavrov expected a new social order to come into being as a result of the transfer of the means of production from the privileged minority to the masses rather than as a result of a transfer of administrative power to a new government or institutions. Like early West European socialists such as Fourier and Robert Owen he was sceptical of the value of political machinations and he shared the view of anarchist compatriots such as Kropotkin and Tolstoy that political power had a corruptive influence on those who wielded it.

The task of persuading the masses to carry out economic and social revolution was urgent, since Russia's progress to a socialism based on its distinctive peasant commune could be jeopardized by the further development of capitalism. Under a limited constitutional monarchy, Lavrov surmised, the Russian bourgeoisie, which at present had no traditions or unity, would grow stronger and the masses would be correspondingly weakened. And yet the means by which the intelligentsia was advised to achieve this objective were ponderous. For Lavrov's strategy gave priority to propaganda over agitation: the revolutionary, he believed, should not attempt to stir up emotions by dwelling on local grievances or particular instances of injustice but should appeal instead to reason by comprehensively explaining the source of the country's ills. To that end the propagandist might have to draw on encyclopaedic knowledge of history, social movements, political theory and even the natural sciences and medicine. However, such protracted self-preparation for propagandistic activity, as Lavrov himself described the task in an article 'Knowledge and Revolution' which was published in *Forward!* in 1873, implied a gradualism that was unattractive to the movement's more impatient spirits [20 *pp. 270–7*]. For them the teachings of Bakunin, who although he was by now an exile like Lavrov enjoyed greater popularity in Russia in the last years of his life than ever before, proved more congenial [127; 129 *ch. 17*].

BAKUNIN

Bakunin, by the 1870s, had long since played a prominent role in European revolutionary politics. In 1842 he had famously concluded his first essay in revolutionary thought, written in Germany under the influence of the radical 'Young Hegelians', with the dictum that the 'passion for destruction is a creative passion' [2 *p. 58*]. In the following years he mixed in France with French and German socialists, including Proudhon and Marx, and with Polish émigrés whose cause of national liberation he supported. He was a participant, in 1848–49, in revolutionary events in Paris and Prague and in an insurrection in Dresden, where he was arrested and whence he was handed over to the Austrian authorities. In 1851 he was extradited to Russia and incarcerated in the Peter and Paul Fortress in St Petersburg. There he wrote a notorious *Confession*, which combined expressions of repentance, appeals for clemency and a *mélange* characteristic of him, of Slav patriotism and Germanophobia. In 1857 he was released to live in Siberia, from which he escaped in 1861. He now travelled, via

Japan and the United States, to Britain, where he was reunited with Herzen, with whom, however, relations shortly deteriorated for political and financial reasons. After a brief stay in Sweden, followed by four years in Italy, he settled in Switzerland and there he continued to attract an international circle of followers and to hatch revolutionary plots until his death in 1876.

While Lavrov affected the revolutionary youth through his appeals to its conscience, Bakunin stirred it by the intrinsic rebelliousness of his thought, by his glorification of revolt and by his personal example as a revolutionary veteran of international renown. For Bakunin, by the end of his life, had established himself as one of the major representatives of anarchism, a doctrine which rejects the state, with its apparatus of army, bureaucracy, laws, judiciary and socially binding institutions such as the Church and the family and which necessarily rests – given its assumption that people are capable of living in harmony without such external coercive apparatus – on a view of human nature as essentially good. Bakunin's anarchism – which is of a very different character to that of Tolstoy (see pp. 85–8) – took clear form during the last years of his life following his escape from Russia and his rift with Herzen. Although his writings are for the most part as fragmentary and as adversely affected by his want of organizational ability as are the numerous networks he seems to have attempted to create, his late work *Statism and Anarchy* (1873) [3] does clearly reflect this hostility to the state in all its forms. He here condemns the theocratic state, the bourgeois state, the autocratic state (as exemplified by tsarist Russia, whose corrupt, authoritarian administration, headed by representatives of a Germanic dynasty, Bakunin was fond of contrasting with the simple, free-spirited Russian people), and even the prospective socialist state (as represented by the dictatorship of the proletariat envisaged by Marx and Engels). This antipathy to authoritarian socialism brought Bakunin, by the end of the 1860s, into destructive conflict with the no less wilful Marx, who contrived to have Bakunin and his libertarian followers expelled from The First International Working Men's Association, which had been founded in 1864, at the organization's congress at The Hague in 1872.

As an anarchist Bakunin could agree with Lavrov that Russian revolutionaries should seek to change society not from above, by the establishment of a revolutionary state and creation of new political institutions, but by helping the people to introduce their own forms of association from below. Like Lavrov he too urged the intelligentsia to move closer to the masses; indeed he suggested that it was the destiny of the intelligentsia now to merge with the masses and to live for them. However, the ultimate object of going to the people, as Bakunin envisaged it, was very different from that conceived by Lavrov. For the masses, as Bakunin perceived them, were not a blank sheet of paper, some *tabula rasa* on which the members of the intelligentsia could inscribe their own favourite thoughts. In a pamphlet of 1862, in which he had contrasted the political order, or lack of it, associated with the Romanov tsars, the leader of peasant revolt Pugachov (see p. 5) and the authoritarian Decembrist Pestel (see pp. 16–19), Bakunin spoke of the Russian people as having untainted ideals of their own: free of the religious, political, legal and social prejudices ingrained in the West and embodied in Western law, the Russian common people would create a new civilization. The task of the intelligentsia should therefore be merely to help the people to express their will, to realize the ideals they had always had but of which they were perhaps not fully aware. This broad strategy found its definitive expression in an appendix to *Statism and Anarchy*, which was very widely circulated among Russian revolutionaries in the 1870s. Since the intelligentsia was unable to teach the masses anything of use, Bakunin argued here in opposition to Lavrov, there was no point in opening 'sociological faculties in the countryside': the peasant would not understand the propagandist and in any case the government would not allow the propagandist to operate. And yet conditions were not unpropitious for revolution. The common people did possess a tripartite socialist and anarchist ideal upon which social revolution could be based. The prime purpose of revolutionaries who went to the countryside should be to break down obstacles to full implementation of this ideal [*Doc. 19*] [*3 pp. 198–217; 20 pp. 278–85*]. The revolutionaries should conduct not propaganda but agitation with a view to fomenting a peasant revolt of the sort to which the Russian people were always prone, as demonstrated, Bakunin believed, by the uprisings of Stenka Razin and Pugachov and even by a proclivity to brigandage which Bakunin admired [110; 124; 129 *ch. 17*; 131 *ch. 6*].

TKACHOV

There is one further revolutionary strategist, Tkachov, who must be examined at this point, although he had little perceptible influence on the revolutionary movement during the 1870s. For Tkachov put forward a strategy that contrasts markedly with those of Lavrov and Bakunin and seems in the light of the revolutionary events of the 1870s, when those strategies were tested, to take more account than theirs of Russian reality. Moreover, Tkachov's thought is often held to prefigure, perhaps even to influence, the strategy later adopted by Lenin. Arrested and sentenced to internal exile for his part in the student disorders of 1868–69, Tkachov escaped abroad in 1873 and settled in Switzerland, where he set up a revolutionary journal of his own, *The Tocsin* (*Nabat*), twenty numbers of which came out between 1875 and 1881.

On one level Tkachov endorsed the Chernyshevskian determinism from which the so-called 'subjective sociologists' Lavrov and Mikhailovsky had taken pains to free radical thought. Tkachov followed Marx – he was one of the first Russian thinkers to make an approving reference to the German socialist – in asserting that people and their culture were shaped by environment, and in particular by economic conditions, and in denying that ideas in themselves had much effect on historical development. And yet at the same time he doubted whether history was governed by laws as rigid as those of the natural sciences, acknowledged the existence in humans of a critical faculty that enhanced their capacity to effect social change, and conceded that a small minority of people might be spurred to action by moral ideals. These deterministic and voluntarist tendencies co-exist uneasily in a review published in 1868 of a book dealing with peasant movements in sixteenth-century Germany. Economic 'principles' governed social orders and it was not possible to disrupt their logical development, Tkachov argued here in his deterministic vein; consequently one could not accomplish far-reaching social change by quickening or slowing the operation of that principle. It might be possible, on the other hand, entirely to alter the governing principle of a society, to replace it with a new one, to accomplish a 'historical leap' from one social order to another.

Tkachov agreed with Lavrov and Bakunin that in the 1870s the conditions for revolution in Russia were favourable but might quickly become less so. The Russian state, unlike its Western counterparts, did not represent the interests of any social class and had no foundations or support in the Russian social structure, he claimed in an 'open letter' addressed to Engels in 1871; it merely 'hung in the air'. Thus although at a distance it gave an impression of might, the state was so weak, Tkachov believed, that it could easily be overthrown. However, capitalism was developing in the wake of the emancipation of the serfs, and as a powerful, conservative class of peasant landowners and farmers and a commercial and entrepreneurial bourgeoisie came into being so the prospect of revolution would fade. Revolutionaries could therefore not afford to wait. '*Now* or not at all quickly, perhaps *never!*' Tkachov warned impatiently, though as a slogan the warning was somehow lacking. It was time to call the revolutionary intelligentsia to action, as the title of Tkachov's journal, invoking the bell rung to summon people in an emergency, was intended to imply.

On the other hand Tkachov was sharply distinguished from the bulk of his contemporaries in the revolutionary movement by his unflattering view of the Russian peasantry. While he did not deny that an oppressed mass was always 'ready' for revolution, he strongly disagreed with Bakunin's optimistic view of the peasant's nature. To Tkachov the peasantry was a passive, conservative force: its age-old slavery and harsh environment had deprived it of rebelliousness and energy. Thus Tkachov compared the peasants to a snail which has withdrawn defensively into its shell and described them – in a phrase that seemed to echo Hobbes's famous view of human life in the state of nature as 'nasty, brutish and short' – as 'coarse, savage and brutal' and bound to remain so as long as they dwelt in poverty.

It followed from this view of the masses as inert and lacking in a socialist ideal of their own that one could not expect the revolution to be carried out from below by the people themselves and that revolutionaries should not squander time and resources on fruitless propaganda or agitation among the peasantry. The responsibility for initiating and executing revolutionary change lay entirely with a minority from within the intelligentsia. Tkachov therefore developed a strategy known as 'Jacobinism', after the faction led by Robespierre and responsible for the revolutionary dictatorship and terror in France in 1793–94, or 'Blanquism', after the later nineteenth-century French insurrectionist and organizer of secret revolutionary societies, Auguste Blanqui. While the revolutionary minority should not omit to foment the discontent that was ever-present among the masses, its main purpose, according to Tkachov and his small number of followers, would be to seize political power itself, and then to exercise that power in order to re-educate the masses and implement the necessary political, economic and social reforms from above [*Doc. 20*]. In order to carry out a *coup d'état* the revolutionary minority would have to bring to their ranks a degree of discipline and organization of which the freedom-loving majority of Russian revolutionaries in the early 1870s seemed temperamentally and ideologically incapable. Tkachov thus advocated the creation of a centralized, hierarchical organization with strict rules which would have the will, single-mindedness, resolve and discipline to act like a military force. He commended the conspiratorial organizations of Ishutin and Nechaev, unsavoury as they might seem in the 1870s, and the pragmatic Machiavellian morality associated with these organizations: his revolutionary minority, convinced of the rectitude of their cause, would not be squeamish in their choice of methods but would approve or disapprove of actions in proportion as they helped or hindered attainment of their goal [126; 129 *ch. 16*; 130].

THE 'GOING TO THE PEOPLE'

At the beginning of the 1870s a further network of socialist circles sprang up in various higher educational institutions, notably in St Petersburg, Moscow, Kiev and Odessa. Collectively the members of these circles were known as the Chaikovtsy, after one of their leading members Chaikovsky, although the name is somewhat misleading, since Chaikovsky was not in the first instance the principal organizer of the network (Natanson played that role) and did not remain at its centre throughout the period during which it was active. The future anarchist Kropotkin also played an important part in this group, writing its lengthy programmatic document. The Chaikovtsy attached great importance to the collection of a broad range of printed matter – for example, the writings of socialist thinkers, both Russian and foreign; works of history and sociology; appropriate imaginative literature – that might aid the revolutionary intending to conduct propaganda among the people. Such literature would both help prospective propagandists to prepare themselves, as Lavrov advised in his article 'Knowledge and Revolution', and serve as material for reading to and discussion with the masses. The Chaikovtsy also began, in 1871, to carry out discreet propaganda among the factory workers in St Petersburg and continued this ground-breaking activity relatively unimpeded by the police – perhaps because, being novel, it was undetected by them – until arrests began to decimate the group in 1873. The Chaikovtsy deplored the cynical Nechaevan approach to revolutionary activity. They also eschewed the hierarchical, strictly disciplined model of revolutionary organization associated with Nechaev. They favoured instead loose, informal associations of the sort which Chernyshevsky envisaged in *What is to be done?* and which many groups of young men and women had tried to establish in practice in the 1860s, associations bound together only by the mutual respect and trust of their members. They thus reflected a view of the socialist circle as not so much a clandestine political society but rather 'a family of men and women', as Kropotkin described it nostalgically in his memoirs, 'closely united by their common object' [18 ii, *p. 107*].

(This charmingly ingenuous view of the socialist circle in the infancy of the revolutionary movement may be compared to the similarly sanguine view of science held by Chernyshevsky and others who, carried away by the rapid advances in scientific knowledge in the first half of the nineteenth century, seemed not to glimpse the possibility that science could be put to malign as well as benign use.)

The Russian revolutionaries of the early 1870s naturally drew inspiration from the works of Bervi, Lavrov and Bakunin (see pp. 67–72). With their sense of idealism, their respect for the Russian common people, their yearning for action and their optimistic conviction that circumstances were ripe for revolution or that peasant revolt was imminent, these works were in harmony with the mood of young men and women who conceived of themselves, as the Chaikovtsy did, as belonging to a knightly order and preparing to perform a social miracle. Moreover young Russian socialists had before them a contemporary example of revolutionary action, namely the so-called 'Paris Commune'. This republican insurrection, which broke out on 18 March 1871 (NS), in the wake of France's defeat in the Franco-Prussian War, and lasted until 28 May, etched itself in the minds of Russian revolutionaries as an instance of heroic proletarian resistance brutally repressed by the bourgeoisie. In these circumstances the urge on the part of a large section of the student youth to forge a close relationship with the masses became irresistible and in the spring of 1874 the scattered attempts already made to conduct propaganda among urban workers and even among the peasantry gave way to a far more ambitious adventure, a 'going to the people' of the sort that radical thinkers such as Herzen and Bakunin had long been advocating. Some 2,000 young men and women now abandoned the major cities and descended on factories and villages throughout European Russia. They took jobs, if they could acquire them, as teachers, clerks, doctors, midwives, carpenters, joiners, dyers, cobblers or farm labourers and used the access to the common people which such jobs afforded them to try to acquaint the people with socialist teachings, to stir up popular resentment at the shortage of land available to the peasants or at the heavy burden of taxation which they bore, or to teach them revolutionary songs, or simply to engage them in conversation [129 *ch. 18*].

The 'going to the people' had the character almost of a religious movement; indeed participants compared themselves to the first Christians, who had renounced the world in which they lived and dedicated themselves to the struggle with evil. For the 'going to the people' satisfied the thirst for self-sacrifice and spiritual exploit that is so pronounced in Russian thought and that perhaps reflects a search for new secular channels of self-expression now that the Orthodox Church was discredited through its association with the autocratic order. And yet this idealism, in the absence of any political experience or organizational framework, could not undermine the regime. The propagandists ranged widely, appearing, it seems, in thirty-seven provinces. However, they had no co-ordinated plan or agreed message, selected their destinations more or less at random, had no means – given the vastness of the country and its primitive system of transportation – of rapidly communicating with their fellows, and often stayed in a location too briefly to have a significant impact on the peasants living in it. In any case the idealism of the revolutionary youth seems not to have been understood or valued by its intended beneficiaries. Sometimes the revolutionaries' criticisms of the local landowners, *kulaks*, officials and clergy – that is to say the most apparent representatives or supporters of the system that exploited them – were well received. And yet it is clear from their own memoirs (as well as from official documents in which the loyalty of the tsar's subjects might have been exaggerated) that powerful forces – ignorance, prejudice, superstition, gullibility, susceptibility to rumour, self-deprecation, servility, fatalistic indifference, deep-rooted conservatism, in fact the forces of whose existence Tkachov had forewarned his generation of revolutionaries – hindered the realization of revolutionary ambitions. The peasants continued to cling to their religious faith and remained confident that the autocrat himself, the paternalistic 'little father' (*batiushka*), would aid them if only he were aware of their plight, which was concealed from him by the landowners and officials. The propagandists' attempts to win the trust of the people by adopting the dress and demeanour of the peasants and workers, their carefully contrived unkemptness, shabby clothing and demotic coiffure in fact tended to excite suspicion or derision. Their mission proved dangerous as well as frustrating: by the autumn of 1874 some 1,600 of them had been arrested, sometimes with the peasants' assistance or following denunciations of them by the peasants themselves. Many of those arrested, less a few who died in detention, were publicly tried at the so-called 'trial of the 193' held from October 1877 to January 1878 by means of which the authorities hoped to shame the revolutionaries and turn the public against them. Most of the remainder of those propagandists and agitators who had set off for the countryside with such high hopes in the spring of 1874 returned in the autumn to the cities whence they had come, and there they reflected on the reasons for the failure of the 'going to the people' and began to test new tactics.

LAND AND LIBERTY

Despite the abject failure of the 'going to the people' it was force of circumstance rather than conscious adaptation of revolutionary theory that dictated modifications of revolutionary practice in the second half of the 1870s. Towards the end of 1876 the nucleus of a new organization, Land and Liberty, began to emerge in St Petersburg. Land and Liberty remained faithful to fundamental Bakuninist principles. It was reaffirmed, for example, that the Russian people were socialist in character; that the revolutionary organization should give expression to the ideals of the people themselves; that capitalism might be bypassed in Russia; that the Russian revolution, unlike revolutions in the West, would emanate from the countryside; and that the model for the Russian revolution had been provided by the leaders of the great peasant rebellions. Faith in the revolutionary potential of the peasant was undiminished and the blame for the débâcle of 1874 was attributed more to the arrogant intention of the intelligentsia to inculcate their own ideal on the peasantry and to their supposed inability to speak to the peasant in a comprehensible way than to any shortcomings on the part of the peasants themselves.

Consequently revolutionaries again went to the people in the spring of 1878, although they did now attempt to settle in the countryside rather than flit from one village or region to another. They also concentrated their efforts to a greater extent on the Volga region, which they identified as the cradle of the great peasant rebellions of the past and the modern refuge of many communities of Old Believers, the schismatics who sought freedom from government persecution for their religious heterodoxy. In 1877 Bakuninist agitators led by Stefanovich and Deich did enjoy a partial success when at Chigirin in the Ukraine they set about preparing a peasant force for an armed uprising by the ruse of distributing false manifestos, purporting to emanate from the tsar, in which the peasants were urged to revolt against the landowners. Hundreds had been recruited to the cause before the conspiracy was exposed by a drunken peasant. Elsewhere the *buntari*, as the Bakuninist agitators were known, had no more success in stirring the Russian peasantry than the propagandists and agitators of 1874.

While continuing to adhere to old theoretical premises and to pursue a more or less familiar strategy, Land and Liberty did make important organizational innovations which took account of the absence of political freedom and the pervasiveness of surveillance in Russia and which entitle one to describe it as the first Russian revolutionary party. As a result of the efforts of two of its members, Oboleshev and in particular Mikhailov, Land and Liberty was moulded into a centralized and disciplined secret society in which the individual was subordinated to the circle and each circle was subordinated to a sovereign centre with power to order individuals to carry out assignments. It was now explicitly accepted that the end justified the means and even that any member of the organization discovered to have betrayed its secrets would be killed.

Land and Liberty was responsible for tactical as well as organizational innovations. Revolutionaries began to turn their attention to forms of activity that had not seemed to have much significance within the strategic framework of preparing the peasantry for social revolution. They resorted to various forms of agitation to advertise their grievances, broaden their support and deepen discontent. They associated themselves, for example, with the renewed student disturbances in the higher educational institutions in the winter of 1877–78. They mounted demonstrations such as a gathering outside the Kazan Cathedral on Nevsky Prospekt in St Petersburg in December 1876 to honour the memory of political prisoners who had died in exile. They established clandestine printing presses inside Russia and produced numerous proclamations, appeals, leaflets, and five numbers of a substantial revolutionary journal bearing the name of their party. Some members, particularly Plekhanov, continued in the footsteps of the Chaikovtsy, conducting propaganda in small circles in most of the industrial quarters of St Petersburg, where they found their audience more receptive than the peasantry to their message. Their growing interest in the urban workers – who were viewed as a relatively accessible extension of the peasantry rather than as a distinct proletarian class – was indicated by the amount of space devoted to the labour movement in their publications in 1878–79. They also benefited from the public sympathy generated, contrary to the hopes of the government, by the 'trial of the 193' and by the slightly earlier trial, in February and March 1877, of the members of a Pan-Russian Social-Revolutionary Organization, more informally known as the Muscovites, a combination of Russian noblewomen, Georgian socialists and Russian workers who had established a network of circles in Moscow and other towns of the industrial heartland in 1875–76. The 'trial of the 193' and the 'trial of the 50', as the trial of the Muscovites was known, were notable for the severity of the sentences – up to ten years of penal servitude for peaceful propaganda – and the selfless idealism of the defendants, whose speeches, subsequently printed on clandestine presses and widely circulated, themselves constituted a further successful form of revolutionary agitation. Besides student disturbances, demonstrations, the production of seditious literature, propaganda in the factories, and court-room oratory, revolutionaries also developed a growing attachment in the second half of the 1870s to terrorism. This 'disorganizational activity', as the programme of Land and Liberty coyly described it, developed in rather a spontaneous way. The violence began in 1876 in Odessa with the shooting of a police agent who was left for dead, his face disfigured by sulphuric acid. In January 1878 Vera Zasulich shot and wounded General Trepov, the governor of St Petersburg (this act aroused widespread public support and Zasulich was acquitted by a jury). In the same month, in Odessa, Kovalsky set a precedent by putting up armed resistance to arrest. In February Osinsky and others attempted to kill a public prosecutor in Kiev. In May, also in Kiev, Popko killed a secret police officer. In August Kravchinsky stabbed to death the head of the secret police in St Petersburg in broad daylight. In February 1879 Goldenberg fatally wounded the governor of Kharkov, who happened to be a cousin of the anarchist revolutionary Kropotkin.

The revolutionary violence was in the first instance directed at individuals such as informers and police officers who threatened the safety of the revolutionaries or at those responsible for their prosecution and punishment. It quickly gained momentum as each side, authorities and revolutionaries, carried out reprisals for the attacks against it. For revolutionaries frustrated by the impassive peasantry it no doubt gave the illusion of decisive action. The sudden escalation of terrorism in 1878 also suggests a response to the draconian punishments meted out by the authorities at the trials of 1877–78 and to the martial atmosphere and increased hardship, especially in the southern cities, brought about by the Russo-Turkish War of 1877–78. (Even the Turkish enemy, revolutionaries liked to claim, was no more cruel and despotic than the Russian authorities, who were frequently described as, or even compared unfavourably to, *bashi-bazouks*.) The motives advanced for terrorism by the revolutionaries themselves were rather confused but became more grandiose as the tactic became more glamorous. At first terrorism was justified in terms of self-defence, vengeance, revolutionary justice and defence of the honour of the party. The benefits expected to flow from it, as they were rather vaguely defined by Kravchinsky in a pamphlet entitled *A Death for a Death*, included an end to persecution for the expression of political convictions, an amnesty for all political prisoners and an end to official arbitrariness. More extravagant hopes came to be pinned on terrorism, though, by such individuals as Tikhomirov, who argued that it might raise the standing of the party among the masses and stir them to protest, and Morozov, who thought it might severely test the political system and who eulogized the terrorists as free people among millions of slaves. Thus by 1879 some members of Land and Liberty had come to accept the 'political' struggle, the contest with the government apparatus, that their predecessors at the beginning of the 1870s had eschewed. Inevitably they now began to contemplate assassination of the autocrat himself, as the person ultimately responsible for all ills in the Russian state, and to look on tsaricide as not only satisfying a thirst for revolutionary justice but as a spur to an economic crisis and popular discontent that might bring down the regime. The drift towards political terrorism was confirmed by a further unsuccessful attempt, made by Soloviov in April 1879, to shoot Alexander II at close range [129 *ch. 20*].

THE PEOPLE'S WILL, 1879–81

By the spring of 1879 an irreconcilable tension had developed within Land and Liberty between those who wished to follow the traditional Bakuninist path, on the one hand, and the supporters of political terrorism against the government, on the other. Finally a conference was held at Voronezh (preceded by a meeting of the advocates of terrorism at the nearby town of Lipetsk). Formal division was temporarily avoided but unity was precarious and by the autumn two factions were operating independently. One faction, led by Plekhanov and embracing also Akselrod, Aptekman, Deich, Stefanovich, Zasulich and others and operating under a banner suggestive of agrarian revolution, The Black Partition, advocated continued agitation among the peasantry. The other, more numerous faction, which embraced advocates of tsaricide such as Mikhailov, Morozov, Tikhomirov, Vera Figner, Sofia Perovskaia and Zheliabov [125], designated itself The People's Will.

The Black Partition suffered immediate setbacks. Leading members were arrested in Moscow and Kiev and its clandestine press was seized by police early in 1880, whereupon Plekhanov, Deich, Stefanovich and Zasulich fled to Switzerland. In any case the party seemed ineffectual, pursuing as it did a failed strategy, and even disrespectful to terrorism's early martyrs inasmuch as it repudiated a form of struggle for which they had suffered. Some of its members did soon defect to the more dynamic People's Will, accepting a need for some 'push' such as a *coup d'état* in present circumstances, while others, including Aptekman and Plekhanov, diluted their opposition to 'political' struggle.

The People's Will, on the other hand, immediately began vigorous activity on several fronts. Although it was its terrorist campaign that brought the party most renown in revolutionary circles and that most disturbed the authorities, its activity was wide-ranging. Like Land and Liberty the party set up clandestine printing presses and produced its own revolutionary journal, five numbers of which, as well as numerous proclamations and leaflets, appeared during the period of its most intense activity between June 1879 and March 1881. It conducted agitation among the students in the higher educational institutions in all the major cities. It founded or brought under its control circles in the armed forces in St Petersburg and at the nearby Kronshtadt naval base and workers' circles in St Petersburg and Moscow and the Ukrainian cities of Kharkov, Kiev and Odessa. It even produced two numbers of a paper written specifically for the workers. It was in general the policy of the party to concentrate forces where they seemed most effective at a given moment. Therefore in the autumn of 1880 (when crop failure, famine in some Volga provinces and the rising price of bread and growing unemployment in the towns caused some unrest) the party seemed prepared to allocate more resources to work among the masses than it had been thought useful to expend there some months before.

At the same time members of the party made repeated attempts – some of which only much later came to light outside revolutionary circles – to assassinate Alexander II. In autumn 1879 they tunnelled under a railway line on the outskirts of Moscow and on 19 November succeeded in derailing two carriages of a train in which Alexander was mistakenly thought to be travelling. A revolutionary who had obtained a job as a carpenter in the Winter Palace smuggled explosives into the building and on 5 February 1880 managed to detonate a bomb there, killing eleven and wounding fifty-six others, although the tsar – who was receiving a foreign guest in the palace at the time – was uninjured. Early in 1881 the party acquired a cheese shop on a street in St Petersburg and tunnelled under a road down which the tsar was expected to pass. Finally a member of the party did succeed in throwing a bomb at Alexander's carriage as it passed down the Ekaterininsky Canal in St Petersburg on Sunday 1 March 1881 and as the tsar dismounted a second revolutionary threw another bomb, killing himself and mortally wounding Alexander, who died shortly afterwards. Five of those implicated in the assassination – including two of the *de facto* leaders of the organization, Sofia Perovskaia and Zheliabov – were publicly hanged on 3 April.

The motives advanced for this terrorist campaign, like those previously advanced by Land and Liberty, were varied. The campaign was explicitly linked to demands for political freedom and a constitution that would guarantee it. This demand was prominent in two 'political letters' contributed by Mikhailovsky to issues of the party's journal and in the letter sent by the party's Executive Committee to Alexander III after the assassination of his father [*Doc. 21*]. It was also more ambitiously claimed that tsaricide might spark off a popular uprising or altogether topple the autocracy and thus clear away the obstacle that impeded revolutionaries' access to the masses. With this latter end in view the party appropriated as its slogan the admonition of the Ancient Roman statesman and orator Cato, '*Delenda est Carthago!*' ('Carthage must be destroyed'): all progress depended on the destruction of the main enemy.

The People's Will had moved a long way from the essentially Lavrovist and Bakuninist positions that prevailed at the rosy dawn of the large-scale movement a decade earlier. Their organization represented a further development of the centralist, hierarchical and conspiratorial model used by Land and Liberty. They recognized the passivity of the peasantry, in present circumstances at least, and effectively withdrew their forces from the countryside. In describing the autocracy, in their journal, as a 'colossus of iron on feet of clay' and regarding its overthrow as a panacea, they seemed close to the position on the Russian state advanced by Tkachov in his open letter to Engels (see p. 73). They frankly acknowledged the importance of 'political' struggle, became locked in a contest with the state itself and proved willing to contemplate revolution from above by means of seizure of political power following an insurrection. All in all these changes were felt by members of the party themselves to reflect a shift from naive acceptance of bookish theory to hard-learned pragmatism and flexibility. Perhaps we might add that if there were two idealized conceptions that had importance for revolutionaries in the 1870s – the ideal of a pure socialistic peasantry and the ideal of an altruistic active intelligentsia – then it was the latter that had now come to prevail.

It is difficult to assess the significance of the assassination of Alexander II in the history of opposition to autocracy in Russia, because one has to try to weigh practical consequences against symbolic value. In immediate concrete terms the assassination brought no benefit to the revolutionary camp. It provoked no popular uprising or mass disturbance, nor did it wring from the government any concession such as an amnesty for political prisoners, a constitution, or the convocation of a popular assembly. On the contrary, it precipitated numerous arrests which decimated revolutionary networks, gave rise to heightened police vigilance which made even peaceful socialist activity more difficult, brought to the throne a tsar of more conservative temper than Alexander II and ushered in a period of exceptionally conservative government. At the same time the assassination undoubtedly gave autocracy an appearance of vulnerability, glamourized the revolutionaries in some quarters (and even won them some sympathy among the public in Western countries), and produced new martyrs for future generations of revolutionaries to revere and emulate. In the larger perspective it is therefore an event that has significance as a major landmark beyond which perceptions of autocracy in Russia could perhaps never be quite the same again [129 *chs 21–2*; 132 *chs 12–15*; 143 *pp. 26–35*].

7 OPPOSITION AFTER 1881

TOLSTOY

The failure of the assassination of Alexander II to yield any results acceptable to radical public opinion combined with the renewed official reaction to produce an atmosphere of despondency in the Russian intelligentsia in the 1880s. As in the 'dismal seven years' that followed the outbreak of revolutions in Europe in 1848, so again in this decade there was a relative dearth of major works of thought and literature, a dearth only partly explained by the recent death of major writers (Nekrasov in 1877, Dostoevsky in 1881, Turgenev in 1883) and by Tolstoy's rejection of an artistic vocation from around 1880. The collective depression and mood of resignation among the intelligentsia in these years is captured in the early work of Chekhov, whose career as writer of short stories and playwright begins in this decade. The eponymous central character of Chekhov's first play, *Ivanov*, first performed in 1887, a man of the generation which had gone to the people full of hope and optimism in 1874, is aimless, exhausted, crushed and ashamed of his inadequacy and ends by committing suicide. The intelligentsia's former preoccupation with social problems and its commitment to social justice were replaced by a new interest in artists who saw their art as an end in itself, such as Baudelaire and Flaubert, in resurgence of religious belief, especially in more mystical forms, or in a passive indifference to the world nourished by Buddhism. Among those who remained committed to social ideals many pursued them in less impatient and forceful ways than had been fashionable in the 1870s, accepting that the world could not be radically changed all at once and contenting themselves with a policy of 'small deeds', that is to say attempts unobtrusively and patiently to ameliorate conditions over many years if not decades or even generations. Others began to subscribe to Tolstoyism, to which we now turn.

In the late 1870s Tolstoy underwent a profound spiritual crisis which made him question the way he had hitherto lived and reject his literary works to date as merely satisfying a vain craving for renown. Filled with self-loathing at the recollection of his participation in war, duelling and gambling and at his lying, promiscuity and drunkenness, he turned to the writings of scholars, scientists, philosophers, sages and theologians. However, none could provide him with an answer to the questions as to the meaning and purpose of life which tormented him; all his enquiries seemed only to point to the conclusion that all is vanity, that death is better than life, and that we must rid ourselves of life. Turning away from his own class, which condoned the false life he had been living, he thought he found truth in the common people, who seemed to display a simple, firm faith, defined as the force of life, and to live for others. Tolstoy describes this crisis and the suffering it engendered in his *Confession* (written in 1878–79, published in Geneva in 1884) [28]. He now set about a renewed study of the gospels and on the basis of it offered his personal interpretation of the meaning of Christianity, an interpretation which seeks to bring the kingdom of heaven down to earth, placing emphasis on the moral and social justice of Christ's teaching, particularly the Sermon on the Mount, rather than on the revelatory dimension of the gospels and the promise of life in the hereafter. He formulates his own commandments, abjuring anger, lust and binding oaths of allegiance. He attaches cardinal importance to the passage in the gospels in which Christ counsels the man who is struck to turn the other cheek in order that his attacker may strike again. For aggressors degrade themselves, Tolstoy believes, by resorting to violence; the most effective way of eradicating the evil they do is not to counter it by similar means but to react with a humility that compels them to shrink in horror from such actions. This pacifism also finds expression in forms more threatening to the state, such as condemnation of capital punishment and repudiation of war – which Tolstoy had experienced at first hand in the Crimea and memorably described in his *Sevastopol Sketches* (1855–56) – with its bloodshed and its capacity to arouse men's ambition.

Once he had undergone this conversion Tolstoy became first and foremost a moralist rather than an artist. The artistic credo of his later years is described in *What is Art?* (1897) [30]: he now requires of art that it 'infect' the subject with the artist's purpose, particularly religious purpose, and rejects his own great novels *War and Peace* (1865–69) and *Anna Karenina* (1875–77) as bad art. After 1880 he produced relatively few works which compete with his earlier writings in terms of artistry. On the other hand he did pen many tracts, such as *What I believe* (written in 1883, banned 1884) and *The Kingdom of God is within You* (1894) [29], and his final novel, *Resurrection*

(1899), in which he outlined the beliefs he now held (elements of which are already present in his earlier writings). He now preached an ethical anarchism, rejecting the coercive state [*Doc. 23*], the official Church, the institution of private property, the oppressive and unjust legal system and the harsh penal system.

In the most general terms Tolstoy after about 1880 urges people to abandon evil ways and live better lives. For it is only through the internal moral improvement of each individual, he believes, not through external, institutional change, that substantial social progress will come about. He hopes that all people – like the eponymous hero of 'The Death of Ivan Ilich' (1886), an ambitious judge, who when he realizes he is dying undergoes a religious conversion – will perceive the falsehood of the goals of rank, wealth and social status which they pursue. The antidote to the ills Tolstoy sees among the upper classes lies in a continuing search for the Rousseauesque natural man glimpsed in his early story 'The Cossacks' (1863) and in a desire to emulate the simple life of the common people, who already in *Anna Karenina* have been depicted as more closely in touch with nature and with themselves than the corrupted inhabitants of the *beau monde* of Moscow and St Petersburg. In search of purity and simplicity the former sensualist now counselled sexual abstinence and vegetarianism, deplored the use of tobacco and alcohol, wore simple clothes and sought as far as possible to become independent of the labour of others, himself working in the fields and making his own boots. Disciples flocked to his estate at Iasnaia Poliana to talk with him and they set up colonies designed to implement his precepts.

Tolstoyism, with its rejection of violence as a means of combating evil, constituted a threat to the revolutionary movement, some of whose representatives complained of the tendency of Tolstoy's teachings to hinder their attempts to recruit the youth for their own purposes in the 1880s. Tolstoy, for his part, abhorred the dogmatism of revolutionaries and their willingness to resort to force. Fictitious examples of revolutionaries, for all their commitment and resolution in the face of punishment, are not presented in a uniformly sympathetic light in *Resurrection*. And yet it would be wrong to see this hostility to the revolutionary camp as diminishing the effectiveness of Tolstoy's personal contribution to the erosion of the authority of the autocratic government. The banning of his tract *What I believe* is indicative of the subversiveness of its content, and the extent of the danger Tolstoy was felt to pose to the official Church is reflected in his excommunication in 1901. His role in undermining the moral legitimacy of the regime under which he lived is paralleled in more recent times by that of Gandhi, who much admired Tolstoy's teachings, and in the Soviet Union by that of Solzhenitsyn [131 *ch. 8*; 134; 135].

PLEKHANOV AND THE 'EMANCIPATION OF LABOUR' GROUP

Arguably the most ominous developments in the 1880s, from the point of view of the tsarist government, were taking place outside Russia itself. As a result of the tradition of political emigration begun by Herzen and Bakunin and continued by Lavrov, Tkachov and many others in subsequent decades, there were well-established Russian communities in such countries as Switzerland, France and Britain where the political climate was freer.

In international anarchist circles Kropotkin, a member of the Chaikovsky circles in the early 1870s (see p. 75), had become prominent as a result of years of agitation in Switzerland and France before settling in England in 1886. In opposition to Darwin, Kropotkin posited mutual aid, not competition and a struggle for survival, as a crucial factor in the natural evolutionary process, and argued for a corresponding social model. However, his major writings (*The Conquest of Bread* (1892) [17] and *Mutual Aid* (1902)) were yet to appear and in the 1880s his influence on the Russian revolutionary movement was negligible [131 *ch. 7*; 141; 150].

Of much greater importance, both in the short term and the long term, were Plekhanov and other former members of Land and Liberty – Akselrod, Deich, and Vera Zasulich – who in 1879, retaining faith in the Bakuninist strategy of attempting to raise a peasant revolt, had aligned themselves with The Black Partition rather than The People's Will but who shortly thereafter had emigrated to Switzerland. Assisted by a wealthy sympathizer, Ignatov, in 1883 they established the so-called 'Emancipation of Labour' Group, dedicated to the popularization of Marxism, to which Plekhanov had now been converted. This task entailed composition of original works making the case for acceptance of Marxism as a doctrine applicable in Russian conditions, production of Marxist works for a Russian readership, organization of transportation of this material into Russia, and maintenance of contacts with socialist groups still active inside Russia.

The two major works which mark Plekhanov's conversion to Marxism are *Socialism and Political Struggle* (1883) and, most importantly, *Our Differences* (1885) [24 i]. Large parts of these works are devoted to polemic with the Populist camp, particularly with the epigones of The People's Will among whom a Jacobin ten-

dency had become pronounced after the assassination of Alexander II.
However, alongside the negative, polemical thread of these works ran
Plekhanov's argument that historical development everywhere followed those same economic and social laws which Marx had discovered and that Russia, while it lagged far behind Western European
countries, was therefore following the same path as those countries.
Nor could societies leap over certain phases of development, so Plekhanov's argument ran, although an understanding of the laws of
development might help them to shorten a phase or alleviate the pains
associated with it. It followed, *pace* Populists of all complexions, that
Russia, on its way to socialism, was bound to pass through a capitalist phase of development. Plekhanov supported his case in *Our Differences* by painstaking examination of the state of Russian industry.
He produced copious evidence to show that the number of factory
workers was increasing, that cottage industries were being transformed into larger-scale forms of production, and that capitalism was
undermining the peasant commune, which Populists continued to
cherish, by splitting the rural community into one stratum of peasants
who were accumulating land and another, larger, stratum which
found itself on the labour market. Plekhanov concluded that capitalism was inexorably gaining ground in Russia, ousting small produc-
ers, driving landless peasants off the land and creating an army of
workers as it had in the West [*Doc. 24*] [133 *chs 5–8*; 143 *ch. 4*].
    The question as to whether capitalism was developing in Russia
and as to its probable future there, while at first sight possibly arcane,
in fact had immense practical significance for Russian revolutionaries
in the last twenty years of the nineteenth century. For if Russia was
indeed following the same capitalist path down which the West had
long since been proceeding, then the Populist notion of national
distinctiveness was mistaken and the Marxist schema was indeed
applicable to Russia. In that event revolutionaries were right to concentrate their attention on the potentially revolutionary proletariat
rather than the peasantry (conceived by Marx and Engels as a
benighted, idiotic class). At the same time it would have to be
accepted that socialist revolution was not an immediate prospect in
Russia and that Russian revolutionaries, while cultivating a socialist
consciousness among the workers, would need simultaneously to co-
operate with the bourgeoisie in fighting the common enemy, autocracy, with a view to winning political freedoms.
    It should be borne in mind when assessing the importance of the
'Emancipation of Labour' Group that Russian thinkers before 1883
were by no means unacquainted with Marx's ideas or dismissive of

them. The first Russian translation of *The Communist Manifesto*, done by Bakunin, had appeared in 1869 and the translation of Marx's *magnum opus*, the first volume of *Capital* (1867), had been completed and published in 1872 (over a decade before its first translation into English). It was not disputed by Russian socialists that Marx had provided a penetrating analysis of the economic system underlying the detested bourgeois order in Western Europe. However, what was not accepted before 1883 was that the laws of historical development that Marx outlined might be applicable to Russia, a relatively backward rural country for which socialists ever since the Petrashevtsy and Herzen had predicted a distinctive historical path that would bypass capitalism. The country was relatively undeveloped industrially, its bourgeoisie was incoherent as a class and politically weak and its small working class could hardly be described as a proletariat, since in most places workers' links with the villages in which they originated were not broken. Even Marx and Engels themselves – who incidentally admired the terrorist struggle of The People's Will against the autocracy – seemed to strengthen the Populist case when in 1882 they wrote a preface to a new, second Russian edition of *The Communist Manifesto* in which they countenanced the possibility, to put it no more strongly, that Russia might indeed be exempted from the laws applicable in the West and might build a form of socialism based on the indigenous peasant commune [*Doc. 22*].

The arguments that could be made for and against acceptance of Marxism as a doctrine applicable to Russia in the 1880s, as they presented themselves to Plekhanov's contemporaries, must have seemed quite evenly balanced. It was to the credit of Marxism, in an age when the efforts of seemingly heroic individuals to topple autocracy had failed, that it placed emphasis on the contest of whole classes as the moving force in the historical process and correspondingly reduced the responsibility on individual agents for the direction which that process took. Moreover, the promise that Marxism seemed to offer that the capitalist order would eventually be undermined by its own contradictions and that socialism would more or less inevitably triumph was reassuring to an intelligentsia now depressed by evidence of its impotence. Finally, it was apparent – particularly in St Petersburg, in Moscow and surrounding towns such as Ivanovo, and in Ukrainian cities such as Kiev, Kharkov and Ekaterinoslav – that industry in Russia was indeed developing in the 1880s and that a working class, whose representatives revolutionaries had long since found more receptive to their propaganda than the peasantry, was therefore growing. On the other hand it counted against Marxism that revolution in the Marxist schema was a long-term prospect, not an immediate one, a goal that would be attained only after a more or less protracted stage of capitalist development during which the misery of the masses would be prolonged and would assume new forms. The more compassionate spirits in the socialist camp found it hard to turn their backs on the suffering of the present generation in the hope of a better life in a distant future. They also found it distasteful to collaborate in the short term with the detested bourgeoisie, as the Marxist schema dictated. Furthermore, abandonment of the path that had been followed for so long seemed to many to imply a betrayal of the movement's martyrs. In any case the beliefs on which Populism rested – that the Russian peasant was innately socialistic, that socialism could be built on the peasant commune, and that Russia could bypass capitalism – had deep roots and a long history in Russian thought. For all these reasons Marxism may have been attractive in intellectual terms but from a moral and emotional point of view – and it was this viewpoint, perhaps, that tended to carry most weight with the intelligentsia in nineteenth-century Russia – Populism remained compelling to most revolutionaries active inside Russia in the 1880s.

It was perhaps indicative of the fact that the climate was still unpropitious for the reception of Marxist ideas in Russia in the middle of the 1880s that the émigré group chose for themselves a name which avoided reference to Social Democracy and that in the first draft of their programme they conceded the need for political terrorism, as if in acknowledgement of the continuing popularity of The People's Will. In any case the group soon suffered a severe organizational setback: in 1884 German police arrested and extradited Deich, the member on whom the group most depended for maintenance of contact with revolutionaries in Russia. And yet if the immediate impact of the group in Russia was small, its importance in the longer term was very great. For Plekhanov had made a crucial contribution to the controversy over capitalism in Russia and had rehearsed the arguments in favour of acceptance of Marxism there, and the group as a whole had established the beginnings of a Russian Marxist literature. Foundations had been laid on which socialists inside Russia were able to build in the 1890s, by which time there was a greater readiness in the intelligentsia to look critically at the weaknesses and failures of Populism [133; 143 *ch. 4*].

REVOLUTIONARY GROUPS IN THE 1880s

The resilience of the old Populist beliefs after the assassination of Alexander II is indicated by the continued appearance of works by imaginative writers such as Zlatovratsky and by publicists such as Kablits (who wrote under the pseudonym Iuzov) which praised the robust peasant or uncritically extolled the collective principles supposedly embodied in the village community. Equally important, the view that Russia was following a separate path of development, or could continue to follow a separate path, was also reasserted, with apparent academic authority, by respected economists. Vorontsov, in an influential book entitled *The Fate of Capitalism in Russia* (1882), doubted whether capitalism was likely to flourish in Russia where he detected a complex pattern of modes of production of which capitalism was only one. Capitalism was an alien growth in Russia, Vorontsov argued, and conditions did not favour its further development: the market was weak, the country was immense and communications were poor, and the entrepreneur's overheads were relatively high owing to the need to provide workers with adequate heating, food and clothing during the severe winter. Iuzhakov, also writing in 1882, argued on the basis of an examination of different types of agricultural production that only a small proportion of land in Russia was utilized according to a capitalist system and agreed with Vorontsov that prerequisites for capitalism's growth, such as the availability of plentiful capital and a proletariat, were lacking. A third economist, Danielson, did accept that Russia's economy was being transformed into a capitalist one but contended that this development could and should be halted [143 *pp. 79–81*; 149].

The majority of revolutionary groups – and such groups did continue to spring up and proliferate, in spite of the repressive climate and official vigilance – also continued to repeat many of the shibboleths of Russian socialists over the preceding decades, although their socialism was often eclectic and confused. For the sake of convenience we may identify three types of group active in the 1880s: firstly, remnants of The People's Will or groups that tried to revive that party or to uphold its tradition; secondly, groups of vaguely Populist character for which theoretical alignment was less important than commitment to patient, 'preparatory' activity that was not expected to yield rapid results; and thirdly, groups that leaned in the direction of one form or another of Social Democracy. These types of group will be examined in order. However, it must be emphasized that this classification is somewhat artificial, for both the political complexion of most of the socialist groups active in the 1880s and the boundaries between the different types of group were unclear.

Repeated short-lived attempts were made after the assassination of Alexander II to reorganize The People's Will. However, these attempts generally betrayed the weakness of the party and indicated that in practice it was no longer mainly preoccupied with, or capable of, a terrorist campaign against autocracy. Some members of the party, for example, in desperation seized upon the anti-Semitic pogroms which broke out in 1881, with official connivance, as encouraging manifestations of a mass revolutionary movement. At the end of that year and the beginning of 1882 the Jacobin tendency in the party, represented by Tikhomirov and Oshanina, came to the fore and leaders of the party advocated a *coup d'état* (although in practice they had no means of carrying it out). The party also found itself forced to beat a retreat from St Petersburg and Moscow, where its declared strategy of political struggle with the government really dictated that it should have its headquarters. Consequently the party often found itself marginalized in distant provincial cities far from the capitals such as Kharkov (where Vera Figner, the last major figure of the party in its heyday to remain at large, was arrested early in 1883) or even isolated backwaters such as Ekaterinoslav, Novocherkassk, Taganrog and Tula, where mainly Jewish revolutionaries (Orzhikh, Bogoraz and others) attempted to restore the party in 1885-86. In such peripheral bases The People's Will found itself pursuing objectives which from the point of view of the authorities seemed relatively innocuous by comparison with political terrorism. In particular the party began to pay increasing attention after 1 March 1881 to propaganda among factory workers in St Petersburg, Kharkov, Kiev, Odessa and even more remote towns such as Ekaterinoslav and Rostov-on-Don.

The desire to give propaganda among the factory workers the theoretical status that its current prominence in practice seemed to merit, as well as resentment on the part of activists inside Russia at the claims to authority made by Tikhomirov and Oshanina, who were now in Parisian emigration, gave rise in 1884 to a dispute between so-called 'young' and 'old' factions of The People's Will. The 'young' faction was represented chiefly by Iakubovich and the 'old' faction chiefly by Lopatin, the émigrés' emissary. The priority attached to propaganda among the workers by the 'young' faction was reflected in their wish to broaden the party's base and to relax the centralist organizational principle in order that greater freedom be given to local groups. The 'young' faction also expressed a preference for 'economic' terrorism – that is to say, attacks on, for instance, harsh factory owners – as against the attempts at tsaricide with which the party had hitherto been associated. In the event, though, further arrests –

made possible by the carelessness of Lopatin – decimated the party towards the end of 1884.

Finally, at the end of 1886, out of the numerous circles that had been formed among the students of St Petersburg, a group emerged which designated itself the 'terrorist faction of the People's Will Party' and which produced bombs with the intention of assassinating Alexander III. Members of the group were arrested on 1 March 1887, the sixth anniversary of the assassination of Alexander II, as they began to patrol Nevsky Prospekt for a third time in the hope of finding their quarry, and on 8 May five of the conspirators – Andreiushkin, Generalov, Osipanov, Shevyriov and Aleksandr Ulianov – were hanged. The programme which Ulianov drew up for this 'terrorist faction' confirmed the interest of supporters of The People's Will in the working class, viewing it as the natural bearer of socialist ideas, speaking of workers as the nucleus of the party and envisaging propaganda and organization in the factories as the revolutionaries' principal task. And yet at the same time the terrorist plot of 1886–87 showed again that the banner of The People's Will remained the rallying-point for the movement's most active spirits [142 *chs 2, 4, 6*; 143 *ch. 2*].

While The People's Will was in its death throes, numerous groups began to devote themselves to patient, careful preparatory work in 'self-education' circles with a view to long-term activity among the workers and peasants and within the intelligentsia itself. One such group was the Muscovite 'Society of Translators and Publishers' which in 1883-84 set about translating and reproducing writings by foreign socialists, including Louis Blanc, Lassalle, Marx and Engels. Other groups sprang up and persisted throughout the 1880s in the main provincial cities with higher educational institutions. In Kazan, a tightly-organized network of circles was developed by the students Fokin, Bekariukov and others, in which members made a careful study of socialist works according to a systematic reading programme, using texts from clandestine libraries and so meticulously observing the rules of secrecy on which Fokin and Bekariukov insisted that the network probably remained intact for almost a decade. Similar networks were established by Fokin in the higher educational institutions of Kiev, to which he moved in 1884, and by Bekariukov when in 1886, on completion of his medical studies, he returned to Kharkov, where fruitful contact was established with local workers' circles. Even the members of such groups themselves found the groups' position on the political spectrum hard to plot. Often they embraced theoretical supporters of various factions, ranging from The People's Will and 'militarists' (who believed in the need to build a

strong organization in the armed forces) to early sympathizers with
Social Democracy and latter-day members of The Black Partition.
(A group of the latter, based in Kazan, produced a symposium entitled
The Social Question (1888) which was indicative of the general confusion at this period: one contributor acknowledged the progress of
capitalism and its impact on the peasant commune but clung to the
dream of peasant revolution.) However, such differences had little significance given that the immediate task, it was generally agreed, was
to gather forces and create a strong organizational base prior to any
future attempt to go to the peasants or workers [142 *chs* 5, 8; 143 *ch.* 3].
At the same time there appeared a number of groups which looked
beyond Populism to Western European examples for socialists to
emulate. The first such group was the 'Party of Russian Social
Democrats', more widely known as the Blagoevtsy after one of the
group's leaders, Blagoev, a Bulgarian student at the University of St
Petersburg (who subsequently became prominent in the socialist
movement in his own country). The group existed from late 1883 to
the beginning of 1887, although by the early months of 1886 it had
already been severely weakened by arrests. The Blagoevtsy devoted
themselves above all to propaganda among the workers in various
regions of St Petersburg and to activities designed to support this
activity such as the acquisition and operation of printing presses, production of a newspaper, and maintenance of a clandestine library of
suitable prohibited literature. They established contact with the émigrés of the 'Emancipation of Labour' Group and in 1886 received a
shipment of literature from them. However, despite their obvious
affinities with the émigrés the Blagoevtsy were not unequivocal supporters of Marxism. Rather their programme – especially their declaration of faith in a democratically elected body expressing the wishes
of the majority – reflected the influence of Marx's rival within the
German Social-Democratic movement, Lassalle. Nor was their thinking free of Populist assumptions. They continued, for example, to
view the peasantry in Russia as an important revolutionary force and
to see the workers as a bridge to the peasantry; they did not altogether
repudiate terrorism; they had links and affinities with the 'young' faction of The People's Will; and works by such authors as Chernyshevsky, Lavrov, Mikhailovsky and Bervi-Flerovsky appeared on
their programme of reading for propaganda among the workers [142
ch. 3; 143 *ch.* 4].
  A further organization that seems to have leaned in the direction of
Social Democracy was a group led by Tochissky which came to be
known as the Association of St Petersburg Artisans and which oper-

ated independently of the Blagoev group among the St Petersburg workers in the period 1885–88. Tochissky maintained a sharp distinction between his group of educated propagandists, on the one hand, and the workers' circles which his Association assisted, on the other. (The workers' circles were partly the product of a labour movement that was beginning to acquire a momentum of its own.) Tochissky – who in the manner of the propagandists of the 1870s tried to lead a simple, ascetic life, dressing like a worker and living in poverty – viewed the intelligentsia as a potentially corruptible force which would only be a temporary ally of the workers, albeit an ally that was necessary to the workers so long as the workers were not fully aware of their own interests. The aim of the Association – and perhaps in this respect Tochissky was influenced by the example of British trade unionism – may have been gradual improvement of the economic conditions of the workers. Its practical activity, however, seems to have been largely pedagogical, a factor that accounts for the relatively light sentences meted out to its members when they were apprehended by the authorities [142 *ch. 3*; 143 *ch. 4*].

There also developed in St Petersburg, in the period 1889–92, a larger network of circles led by Russian student leaders, notably Brusnev and Krasin (a future Soviet ambassador in London), and a number of Polish students. These circles too conducted propaganda among the factory workers of the capital and participated in various forms of agitation such as promotion of strikes, production of a workers' paper, and arrangement of May Day meetings in 1891 and 1892. Here too the emphasis seems to have been on careful preparation for a long-term campaign that might yield solid results in the distant future. It is debatable, though, to what extent the workers were primarily interested on the whole in formation of economic associations or political organizations rather than in educational and personal self-improvement and even to what extent they welcomed their association with these representatives of the intelligentsia [143 *pp. 155–60*; 145]. Even in provincial cities groups with Marxist leanings were now appearing. The earliest such grouping was that led by Fedoseev who briefly enjoyed influence in student circles in Kazan in 1888–89. Fedoseev had embarked on a plan to acquire and have translated and reproduced several texts from the Marxist canon when he was arrested. It was probably at this time that the future Lenin, younger brother of Aleksandr Ulianov and himself expelled from Kazan University for his part in student demonstrations there late in 1887, first became acquainted with Marx's *Capital*, although until his departure from Kazan in the spring of 1889 he was almost certainly more sympathetic to the tradition of The People's Will, for which Aleksandr had laid down his life, than to the alien stream of socialist thought [142 *chs 7-8; 143 pp. 99–107, 145–55*].

POLITICAL MOVEMENTS IN THE 1890s

The political conditions in which Russian revolutionaries operated after 1894, when Alexander III died and was replaced by his son Nicholas II, remained essentially the same as in the previous reign. Nicholas promptly scotched hopes of political reform by reaffirming the principle of autocracy upheld by his father and his mentor Pobedonostsev and by rebuking *zemstvo* leaders who had been 'carried away by senseless dreams about participation by representatives of the *zemstvo* in the affairs of internal government' [45 *p. 549*]. And yet the demand for political reform was about to become irresistible. For one thing, in an autocratic state where the will of an individual is supreme, the accession of a new ruler generally heightens the expectation of change. In any case Nicholas, a mild man happiest in the bosom of his family, seemed a less intimidating ruler than his predecessors. Most importantly, under the supervision of the energetic Count Witte, who was Minister of Finance from 1892 to 1903, and with the support of Nicholas himself, Russia's economy underwent rapid modernization in the 1890s. This process – achieved through the attraction of foreign loans and investment, establishment of financial stability, maintenance of protective tariffs, further expansion of the railway network, development of mining in the Ukraine, and growth of grain exports through the Black Sea ports – threw the obsolescence of Russia's political structure into even sharper relief.

In these conditions movements began to develop that were to lead to the proliferation of political organizations and the intensification of political activity in the last years of the nineteenth century and the early years of the twentieth century and eventually to the Revolution of 1905. The principal movements that can be distinguished may be classified as liberal, Populist, and Social-Democratic, although it should be emphasized that the distinctions between them, both ideological and organizational, are not always clear-cut. All these movements represent continuations of the pre-existing streams of opposition to autocracy, or rather the re-emergence and quickening of those streams after a period in which their flow had been sluggish and partly hidden from view.

The liberal movement of the end of the century grew partly out of the efforts long since made by members of the rural intelligentsia to

bring about social improvements at local level within the legal framework provided by the *zemstva*, the councils set up from 1864 in one
of the reforms that followed the emancipation of the serfs. In the
1880s such activity accorded well with the policy of 'small deeds',
with which many members of the intelligentsia, bereft of great expectations, were then content. (This modest policy has an echo in the
plays of Chekhov, with their characters resigned to the present stagnation but hopeful that their descendants might one day live more satisfying lives.) At the level of the so-called 'third element', that is to say
hired professional employees of the *zemstva*, the rural intelligentsia
established firm contact with the peasantry in the closing decades of
the century through their positions as doctors, nurses, teachers, veter-
inary surgeons, lawyers and agronomists [144 *p. 7*]. At a higher level,
among the appointed officials of the *zemstva*, there was a desire to
share such local experience of social activity. This desire gave rise to
an aspiration, which might elsewhere have seemed unexceptionable,
for the creation of consultative bodies. Although Shipov [72 *ch. 6*], a
Moscow *zemstvo* leader who most prominently expressed this aspiration, was allowed to organize such a meeting of *zemstvo* provincial
board chairmen at Nizhnii Novgorod in 1896, he was not permitted
to repeat the exercise in St Petersburg the following year. A bolder
strand of liberalism gave rise at the beginning of the twentieth century
to the establishment of a paper, *Liberation* (*Osvobozhdenie*) in Stutt-
gart under the editorship of Struve and the foundation of an illegal
opposition party, the Union of Liberation, chaired by Petrunkevich
and dedicated to the abolition of autocracy and establishment of constitutional government [45 *pp. 553–7*; *101*].

As for Populism, it was reinvigorated in the 1890s by dismay at the
severe famine which afflicted the central black-earth provinces in
1891 and which was followed by an outbreak of cholera and peasant
unrest. This rural crisis revived the desire on the part of the urban intelligentsia to go to the aid of the peasant mass, precipitated a return to
the people, for humanitarian purposes, and thus led to renewal of that
contact with the peasantry which the revolutionaries of the 1870s had
tried to establish. The crisis also vividly highlighted for revolutionaries the question – which was bound to be answered as much on emotional as on purely rational grounds – as to whether the intelligentsia
should concentrate on the alleviation of present hardship or dedicate
itself to struggle for eventual political change which would supposedly remove the causes of such hardship in the longer term.

The mouthpiece for 'legal Populists' in the 1890s was the journal
Russian Wealth (*Russkoe bogatstvo*) and its main spokesman the

indefatigable Mikhailovsky, who in 1894 produced an emotional critique of Marxism. Attempts to revive a Populist movement were made by activists of an earlier period who were now returning from exile such as Natanson, who created a short-lived organization called The People's Right in 1894, and Breshko-Breshkovskaia, one of the propagandists of 1874.

More important were various groups such as the Union of Socialist Revolutionaries, founded in Saratov in 1896 (also known as the 'Northern Union'), which moved its headquarters to Moscow in 1897, and the Southern Party of Socialist Revolutionaries founded in Voronezh in 1897. The Northern Union followed in the tradition of The People's Will, advocating terrorism with the aim of political liberation and neglecting activity among the peasantry, while the Southern Party put forward a strategy more reminiscent of the Black Partition, that is to say agitation among the masses, mainly the urban workers but not excluding the peasantry. Independently of these groups Chernov made attempts in Tambov Province in the period 1895-99 to take revolutionary ideas to the peasantry, placing emphasis, as an earlier generation of Populists had done, on the moral dimension of socialism and even hoping to exploit sectarian antipathy to the authorities [144 *ch.* 2]. A further group, founded in Minsk in 1898 by Breshko-Breshkovskaia and a young Jewish chemist Gershuni, also advocated political terrorism. The foundation of an Agrarian-Socialist League in Paris in 1900 represented an attempt to amalgamate the scattered Populist groups. In the course of 1901–2 these groups merged into the broad Party of Socialist Revolutionaries (the SRs) which was led at this stage by Breshko-Breshkovskaia, Chernov, Gershuni and Natanson among others. The continuing popularity of terrorism was attested by a spate of assassinations, some of them carried out by the so-called Combat Detachment of the SRs, in the early twentieth century.

While Populism struggled to reassert itself, the popularity of Marxism increased rapidly among the intelligentsia in the early 1890s, both in St Petersburg and in provincial backwaters which had recently been Populist strongholds. In 1893 Lenin, having qualified as a lawyer in Samara, where he lived from 1889–1893, joined one of the Marxist circles in St Petersburg and in 1895 went abroad and visited Plekhanov, who had recently strengthened the Russian case for Marxism with a powerful exposition of historical materialism in his work *On the Question of the Monistic View of History* (1894). On his return to St Petersburg Lenin collaborated with Martov (pseudonym of Tsederbaum), a Jewish revolutionary from Vilna (modern Vilnius, capital of Lithuania), to amalgamate the Marxist groups in the capital as a

Union of Struggle for the Liberation of the Working Class, which was however destroyed by arrests in 1895–96. (Both Lenin and Martov were exiled for three years to Siberia, where Lenin produced his own statement of the case for the application of Marxism in Russia, a long study of the penetration of the rural economy by capitalism entitled *The Development of Capitalism in Russia* (1899).) Surviving groups of Marxist intellectuals and workers met secretly at Minsk in 1898 and founded the Russian Social-Democratic Labour Party (RSDLP), but it too was soon incapacitated by arrests.

Within the Marxist camp, however, fissures soon developed that mirrored those in the Populist camp a generation earlier. These fissures concerned such thorny questions as the degree to which socialist activity should take place within the existing legal framework, the relationship between political and economic struggle, and the relationship between the intelligentsia and the masses (now the urban workers rather than the peasantry). Mindful of the successes of Social Democrats in gaining political influence in the freer countries of the West, some Marxists – Berdiaev, Bulgakov, Struve, Tugan-Baranovsky – concentrated their attention on the short-term objective which Marxists shared with the bourgeoisie, namely the winning of political freedoms and the undermining of autocracy [138; 139]. Not surprisingly, some of the 'legal Marxists', as these Marxists came to be known, were later to lean towards the liberal camp and made important contributions to the volume entitled *Landmarks* (1909) which criticized the tendency of the Russian intelligentsia to take up polarized ideological standpoints. A different position was taken by Kremer, another Jewish revolutionary from Vilna, who in his pamphlet *On Agitation* (1894) argued that the intelligentsia should learn from the masses and represent their grievances. According to yet another point of view, adopted by some intellectuals such as Prokopovich and his wife Kuskova, socialists should strive primarily to win for the workers economic gains and material improvements of the sort that it seemed possible to achieve in some Western countries. Yet other socialists of the period, led by Takhtariov and represented in the newspaper *Workers' Thought* (*Rabochaia mysl'*; 1897), continued abroad as *The Workers' Cause* (*Rabochee delo*), were concerned to build a mass labour movement rather than one dominated by Marxists in the intelligentsia. These various heresies, actual or somewhat exaggerated for polemical purposes, are vehemently opposed by Lenin in his work *What is to be done?* (1902) [21]. Taking his title from Chernyshevsky's novel, which he greatly admired, Lenin argues in *What is to be done?* that the working class, if left to its own devices, could achieve only a 'trade-union' consciousness which would bring no durable improvement in its condition. He makes the case for a tightly organized, conspiratorial party, holding up Land and Liberty and The People's Will as examples to be emulated. Such a party would not be a broad-based working-class organization but an organization of active revolutionaries. Thus *What is to be done?* prepares the ground for the split which took place at the second congress of the RSDLP, held in 1902 first in Brussels and then London, as a result of which Russian Social Democrats came to be divided into the factions known as Bolsheviks and Mensheviks [136; 137; 146; 147; 148].

PART THREE: ASSESSMENT

In the late eighteenth century, Russia's nascent educated public, which at that time consisted largely of the Westernized nobility, still conducted debate about matters of cultural, social and political concern without seriously questioning the legitimacy of autocracy as a form of government for the country. However, quite early in the nineteenth century, and partly as a result of Russia's involvement in the Napoleonic Wars, this harmony between civil society and the autocratic state began to break down. As Russia moved closer to the West in cultural terms and played a more prominent part in European political affairs, so her form of government came to seem more akin to an oriental despotism than to polities of the sort with which educated Russians were becoming increasingly familiar through their travels and long stays in Western Europe. Relations between state and educated public were aggravated by the general resistance of autocracy to reform, by a perception that even when reforms were introduced – as after the Crimean War – they did not go far enough, and in particular by the refusal of autocracy to contemplate political reform consistent with the social and economic changes taking place in Russia in the second half of the century. At the same time the eighteenth-century sense that the nobleman had a duty to serve the state – a sense that persisted even after the formal abolition of the obligation to serve in the army, navy or civilian administration in 1762 – was translated into new conceptions of duty, towards such abstractions as art, the Absolute Idea of Hegelian philosophy, and – most subversively – the people.

In the course of the nineteenth century even social groups that had once been generally loyal to autocracy became alienated from it: the parish clergy ceased to see the tsar as the defender of the faith and, at opposite ends of the social spectrum, both nobles and peasants lost faith in the myth of the tsar's benevolence. However, it was principally through the group that came to be known as the intelligentsia that opposition to autocracy was articulated. Or, to put it another way, it was as an 'intelligentsia' that an independent civil society came to conceive of itself. The social composition of the intelligentsia changed considerably during that golden age, from about 1820 to 1880, when Russia's classical literature and thought were being created and when society and state were becoming alienated from one another. Rebellion that in the immediate post-Napoleonic period found expression among the high nobility – the social group from which the Decembrists mainly emanated – was by the middle of the century led by men of various social strata, the *raznochintsy*. The chief loci of opposition moved from the aristocratic drawing room and the officers' mess to the editorial board of the 'thick' journal, the student circle, and the clandestine revolutionary cell. As opposition was democratized and radicalized in these ways women came to play a larger and more prominent part in it. Although in the first half of the century they did frequent and in some cases preside over the salons in which cultural life was conducted, during the second half they became a more powerful presence in the socialist commune or revolutionary circle and suffered punishment together with men for the pilgrimages to the people and the acts of terrorism.

The Russian nineteenth-century intelligentsia, in all the phases of its development, professed an admirable independence, integrity and idealism. Its members placed great faith in the power of ideas and, in the second half of the century, in natural science, which they valued both as an instrument for the improvement of material civilization and for its apparently incontestable method of solving problems of all descriptions. And yet the systems of ideas which the intelligentsia constructed often had a character no less authoritarian than the political and social system against which the intelligentsia was pitted. Moreover, the lack of representative political institutions, the absence of a vigorous free political life and the consequent exclusion of the intelligentsia from government helped to give free rein to a mode of thinking that was unpractical, even irresponsible, as well as idealistic. For there was little real prospect that members of the intelligentsia would themselves have to put the utopian theories which they pressed upon their readers into practice in the imperfect, unpredictable world of human affairs, social relations and historical events.

Divisions within the intelligentsia itself were numerous, and opinions differed greatly as to the course that opposition to autocracy should take. Indeed some thinkers, of conservative persuasion, continued throughout the nineteenth century to defend autocracy as the most appropriate form of government for Russian territory or the

Russian people. (Even thinkers in this tradition – to which the Slavophiles and native-soil conservatives such as Dostoevsky belonged – had reservations, though, about the nineteenth-century state, whose Westernizing bureaucratic apparatus undermined the consensual paternalistic form of autocratic rule that supposedly characterized pre-Petrine Muscovy.) However, as the loyalty of the educated public towards the autocratic state began to dissipate after the Napoleonic Wars, a larger section of the educated class – though still, it should always be remembered, a very small proportion of the population of the country as a whole – tried to define Russia's future not as a re-creation of a distant past but as part of an international social transformation prepared by ideas furnished by the more advanced Western European civilization. The paramount question for members of this camp of the intelligentsia, once the case of conservative nationalists had been answered, was whether to attempt to reform and civilize Russian society within the existing political structure or to seek more radical change, possibly by revolutionary means. Westernizers of the more moderate type, such as the liberal Westernizers of the 1840s and 50s (for example, Granovsky and Kavelin), Chicherin in the reign of Alexander II, and the later liberals working within the *zemstva*, did not directly challenge the autocratic state. Indeed they were more or less convinced that only the survival of a strong autocracy would guarantee preservation of order during a period of reform. On the other hand Westernizers of the more radical type – Belinsky and Herzen in the 1840s, Chernyshevsky, Dobroliubov and Pisarev in the 1850s and 60s – envisaged the establishment of a new social – and moral – order incompatible with the survival of autocratic government. The intellectual rebellion which they set in motion in the 1840s and which culminated in the nihilism of the 1860s precipitated a tide of revolutionary action that abated in the 1880s, only to re-emerge with increasing force, but moving now in various directions, at the end of the century.

Within the revolutionary movement too, divisions quickly became apparent. For one thing, revolutionaries had to decide whether to attempt to replace autocracy by some alternative form of government, perhaps equally authoritarian, as recommended by Tkachov and eventually Lenin, or to abolish government with coercive power altogether, as anarchists such as Bakunin, Kropotkin and Tolstoy advocated. For another, the question of national identity continued to give difficulty. Whereas the first wave of Russian revolutionaries, in the 1870s, identified the supposedly indigenous institution of the peasant commune as a basis for socialism and envisaged progress towards the socialist goal by a separate path from that being taken by Western nations, Russian Marxists, beginning with Plekhanov in the 1880s, viewed Russia as essentially a member, albeit a backward one, of the European family of nations and welcomed signs of the development of a proletariat there.

When due account has been taken of the divisions within the intelligentsia that have been examined in this book, it should all the same be noted that there are qualities and emphases in the thinking of that intelligentsia which tend to cut across the divisions and which lend Russian thought a distinctive character. The Western student might expect Russian thinkers, living under a capricious autocracy, to give high priority to establishment of the rule of law and to protection of the individual from the whim of the autocrat and his favourites. On the whole, however, the mission of these thinkers is a grander, more messianic one, the construction of a social and moral utopia, the realization even of the kingdom of heaven on earth. Their thought has a pronounced utilitarian quality: they come to be dissatisfied with the pursuit of art or philosophy or any branch of culture or knowledge for its own sake and are driven to seek truths that can be readily applied. They display a fierce moral engagement, even religiosity. They tend to subordinate the interest of the individual to that of the larger unit – family, peasant commune, Church, people, nation – which the individual inhabits. Finally, they express a perennial anxiety about national identity and thus provide a model for debate of a sort that recurs throughout the nineteenth and twentieth centuries in developing nations in which Westernization and modernization have imperilled native values and institutions.

PART FOUR: DOCUMENTS

AN EIGHTEENTH-CENTURY VIEW OF
AUTOCRACY

*This extract is taken from a note which Radishchev made in a translation,
done by him in the 1770s, of a work on Ancient Greek history by the contemporary French political writer and philosopher, abbé Mably. The extract
shows Radishchev's yearning for the rule of law and the threat posed to
autocracy by notions such as that of a political contract between rulers and
their subjects.*

Autocracy is the condition most contrary to human nature. Not only can we not
grant unlimited power over ourselves, but neither does the law, that expression of
the popular will, have any right to punish criminals, other than the right of
ensuring that its precepts are not violated. If we live under the authority of the
law, then this is not because we must do so out of necessity, but because we
derive some advantage from it. If we surrender to the law some of the rights
and freedoms to which we are entitled by nature, then we do so in order that
they should be used for our benefit. In this respect we enter into an unspoken
agreement with society. If this agreement is broken then we are freed from our
obligations. An injustice perpetrated by a sovereign ruler gives the people the
same or greater right to judge that ruler as he has under the law to judge criminals. The sovereign is the first citizen of the people's society.

From Leatherbarrow and Offord, [20], p. 17.

DOCUMENT 2   THE CAUSES OF THE DECEMBRIST REVOLT

*The following is an extract from a digest of the testimony given by Decem-
brists during the official investigation into their revolt. It summarizes some of
the reasons for the discontent which led to their mutiny.*

The most brilliant hopes for the prosperity of Russia marked the beginning of
the reign of Emperor Alexander I. The nobility relaxed; the merchants did not

complain about credit; the military served without hardship; scholars studied whatever they wished; everybody could say what they thought; and from the great good of the present everybody expected better things still. Unfortunately, circumstances did not allow this to happen, and the hopes grew old, unfulfilled. The unlucky war of 1807 and other costly campaigns ruined finances. Napoleon invaded Russia and it was then that the Russian people perceived their power, it was then that the feeling for independence – first political, later also national – was kindled in every heart. This was the origin of the ideas of liberty in Russia. The government itself pronounced the words: liberty, liberation. Itself it disseminated works on the abuses of Napoleon's unlimited power. The war was still in progress when the returning soldiers' grumblings first spread among the people: 'We have spilled our blood,' they said, 'but they force us to sweat again at corvée; we have freed the country from the tyrant, but our lords tyrannize us again.' Having returned to the fatherland, the armies – from general down to soldier – continuously spoke of how good it was in foreign lands.

From Marc Raeff, *The Decembrist Movement*, [26], p. 32.

DOCUMENT 3   THE DECEMBRISTS' VIEW OF AUTOCRACY

This is an extract from the introduction to the first draft of the Constitution written in 1821–22 by Nikita Muraviov for the Northern Society (from which many of the Decembrists were to emerge in 1825). In it Muraviov states the case against autocracy and thus establishes a starting point for the plan, outlined in his second draft, for separation of powers and elected legislative assemblies.

The experience of all nations and all epochs has shown that autocratic power is equally ruinous for both rulers and society; it accords with neither the principles of our holy faith nor those of sound reason. One cannot allow the arbitrary rule of one man to become a principle of government. One cannot accept that all rights belong to one side and all duties to the other. Blind obedience can be based only on fear and is worthy of neither a reasonable ruler nor reasonable ministers. By putting themselves above the law sovereigns have forgotten that they are thereby outside the law, outside humanity! They cannot have recourse to the law in matters concerning others and not acknowledge the law's existence when the matter concerns themselves. There are two possibilities: either the laws are just – in which case why do they not wish to submit to them themselves – or they are unjust – in which case why do they subject others to them? All European nations are securing laws and freedom. More than any other the Russian people deserves both.

From Leatherbarrow and Offord, [20], p. 42.

DOCUMENT 4   PESTEL'S 'RUSSIAN LAW'

This extract is taken from the introduction to the legal code drafted (but not completed) by the Decembrist Pestel. In it Pestel sets out in a republican spirit the rules which he believes governments must follow in their quest to promote public well-being, and outlines the basic tasks confronting opponents of autocracy.

The first rule ... is that all the state's efforts in the pursuit of happiness must accord with spiritual and natural laws. The second law is that all state statutes must be directed solely towards the well-being of civil society, and therefore any act contrary to this well-being, or injurious to it, must be considered criminal. The third rule is that the well-being of society must be regarded as more important than individual happiness, and if the two conflict then the former should take priority. The fourth rule is that the well-being of society should be defined as the happiness of the totality of the people, from which it follows that the real aim of a state system must necessarily be the greatest possible good of the greatest number of people in the state. This is why the benefit of the individual part must always yield to the benefit of the whole, the whole being the totality or mass of the people. The fifth and final rule is that the individual, in the pursuit of personal happiness, must not step outside his own area of action and encroach upon the activities of others – in other words, the happiness of one should not bring harm, still less ruin, to another ...

... the Russian people is not the possession or property of any individual or family. On the contrary, the government belongs to the people – it is established for the good of the people, and it is not the people which exists for the good of the government.

... Applying these immutable and indisputable basic principles to Russia it is clear to see that these very principles necessarily demand a change in the existing political order in Russia and its replacement by a structure based solely on precise and just laws and statutes, which will leave nothing to personal and arbitrary will and which will assure the Russian people with complete exactness that it is indeed an organized civil society and not someone's property or possession, which it never can be. From this emerge two main requirements for Russia: first, the complete transformation of the political order and its organization; and second, the publication of a complete new code of laws which will preserve what is of value and eradicate what is harmful.

From Leatherbarrow and Offord, [20], pp. 52–3.

DOCUMENT 5   CHAADAEV'S 'PHILOSOPHICAL LETTER'

Chaadaev's first 'Philosophical Letter' relegated Russia to an insignificant place in the history of human civilization and helped to precipitate the debate between the Slavophiles and Westernizers in the 1840s.

One of the most deplorable features of our peculiar civilization is that we are still only beginning to discover truths which have long been truisms elsewhere, even among nations less advanced in certain respects than we are. This is the result of our never having marched in step with other nations; we belong to none of the great families of mankind; we are neither of the West nor of the East, and we possess the traditions of neither. Standing, as it were, outside time, we have not been touched by the universal education of mankind.

That wonderful intermingling of human ideas through the succession of the centuries, that history of the human spirit which has led man to the heights he has reached today in the rest of the world, has had no effect on us. That which in other lands has long constituted the very basis of social life is still only theory and speculation for us ...

Look around you. Don't we all have one foot in the air? We all look as though we are travelling. No one has a definite sphere of existence; no one has proper habits; there are no rules for anything; there is no home base; everything passes, leaving no trace either outside or within us. In our home we are like visitors, among our families we are like strangers, in our cities we are like nomads, more nomadic than those whose animals graze on our steppes, for they are more attached to their deserts than we are to our cities ...

Cast a glance over all the centuries through which we have lived and over all the land we inhabit – you will find no endearing memory, no venerable monument to speak to you forcefully of the past or allow you to relive it in a vivid and picturesque manner. We live only in the narrowest of presents, without a past and without a future, in the midst of a flat calm. And if we manage to stir ourselves from time to time it is not in the hope of desire for some common good, but with the puerile frivolity of a child who raises himself and stretches out his hands towards the rattle which his nurse offers him.

From Leatherbarrow and Offord, [20], pp. 67–9.

DOCUMENT 6   THE LIBERAL WESTERNIZERS' ASPIRATION
             FOR THE RULE OF LAW

This is an extract from a public lecture on the thirteenth-century French king Louis IX which Granovsky delivered in Moscow University in 1851. The extract illustrates the admiration of the liberal Westernizer for monarchs and jurists who, he thought, gradually transformed the feudal state into one imbued with a sense of law (in its Roman form) and justice.

... Louis IX set an example from which his successors were not to deviate. His decrees concerning judicial duels and private wars underpinned subsequent legislation. The people who helped Louis with these reforms were learned jurists, who enjoyed his especial respect and trust. The reforms of which they were the authors were not of course envisaged by the King, who thought only about the ennoblement and consolidation of feudal institutions through greater justice and morality. He knew that the knights were bad judges and replaced them as far as possible by people who had studied law as a science. The consequences came to light after Louis's death. The jurists whom he had set on a career of practical activity constituted a whole estate inimical to the ideas and forms of the Middle Ages. They opposed the strictly logical and generally applicable decisions of Roman law to the local and idiosyncratic customs which had developed in the states of Western Europe which had been founded by the Germans. They indicted the medieval papacy in the person of Boniface VIII and the spiritual knighthood in the form of the Templars. Feudal gentry and commoners alike felt their influence ... Louis IX could not foresee the political significance which the experts in Roman law subsequently acquired, and valued only their judicial activity. I do not consider it necessary to repeat to you the all too familiar story of Joinville [a chronicler] about how the King, surrounded by men experienced in the science of law, himself resolved the law-suits of his subjects and passed sentences under the famous oak of Vincennes. King and justice became synonymous words for France at that time. In the whole state there was not an impartial judge except for him, because he alone stood outside, or it would be better to say above, all mercenary ambitions. The idea of monarchical power was invested with the moral radiance of incorruptible justice.

From Leatherbarrow and Offord (slightly revised), [20], pp. 175–6.

DOCUMENT 7   BELINSKY'S 'LETTER TO GOGOL'

In 1847 Belinsky castigated the novelist Gogol for giving comfort to the regime in one of his works and for allegedly betraying the independent intelligentsia. In these extracts Belinsky dwells on Russia's acute social problems, the supposedly atheistic nature of the Russian people and the civic responsibility of the writer.

... you know Russia deeply only as an artist and not as a thinker – a role you have assumed so unsuccessfully in your fantastic book. Not that you are not a thinking man, but for so many years you have been accustomed to looking at Russia from your 'beautiful far-away' ... you have failed to notice that Russia sees her salvation not in mysticism, asceticism, or pietism, but in the advances of civilization, enlightenment and humanism. She does not need sermons (she has heard enough of those already!), or prayers (she has repeated them for long enough!), but an awakening in the people of a sense of human dignity, buried for so long in the dirt and the muck. She needs rights and laws compatible with good sense and justice, rather than with the teachings of the Church, and the strictest possible enforcement of them. But instead of this she presents the ghastly spectacle of a country where people traffic in people without even the excuse so cunningly employed by the American plantation owners, who claim that the negro is not a human being; a country where people are not known by names but by nicknames like Vanka, Stioshka, Vaska and Palashka; a land, finally, where not only are there no guaranteed rights of personal integrity, honour, or property, but there is not even a proper police system, only huge corporations of various official thieves and robbers. The most vital national problems in Russia today are the abolition of serfdom, the repeal of corporal punishment, and the strictest possible implementation of at least those laws which do exist ...

According to you the Russian people are the most religious in the world. That is a lie! The basis of religious feeling is pietism, reverence and the fear of God. But the Russian speaks the name of God while scratching his behind. He says of icons: 'if you can't use them for praying, use them for covering the pots.' If you look more closely you will see that these people are by nature profoundly atheistic. They have many superstitions, but no trace of religious feeling. Superstition passes with the progress of civilization, whereas religious feeling often keeps pace with it. A good example is provided by France, where even now there are many sincere and fanatical Catholics among enlightened and educated people, and where many still cling stubbornly to some sort of divinity even though they might have discarded Christianity. The Russian people are not like that: mystical exaltation is not in their nature; they have too much common sense, too clear and positive a mind for that – and therein perhaps lies the greatness of their historical destiny in the future ...

... Only in literature is there life and forward movement, despite the Tatar censorship. That is why the title of writer is so respected among us; that is why literary success comes so easily even to those of limited talent. The titles of poet and writer have long since eclipsed the trumpery of epaulettes and fancy uniforms in Russia ... And here the public is right: it sees in Russian writers its only leaders, its protectors and saviours from the darkness of autocracy, Orthodoxy and nationality, and therefore although it is always prepared to forgive a writer a bad book, it will never forgive him a harmful one.

From Leatherbarrow and Offord, [20], pp. 130–34.

DOCUMENT 8   A FOREIGN TRAVELLER'S VIEW OF THE
                PEASANT COMMUNE

These extracts are taken from a book on the Russian Empire by a Prussian Baron, von Haxthausen, who travelled extensively in Russia in 1843. In them Haxthausen presents the commune as a valuable social institution which he believes will protect Russia from the development of a proletariat and the consequent bane of socialism.

The Communes present an organic coherence and compact social strength which can be found nowhere else, and yield the incalculable advantage that no proletariate [*sic*] can be formed so long as they exist with their present constitution. A man may lose or squander all he possesses, but his children do not inherit his poverty: they still retain their claim upon the land, by a right not derived from him, but from their birth as members of the Commune ...

Russia has thus nothing to fear from the revolutionary tendencies which threaten the rest of Europe. Its own internal healthy organization protects it against pauperism, and the doctrines of communism and socialism. In the other modern states, pauperism and proletarianism are the festering sores to which the present condition of society has given birth.

From Haxthausen, [12], vol. i, pp. 123–4, 135.

DOCUMENT 9   HERZEN ON THE RUSSIAN PEASANT

This is an extract from an 'open letter' which Herzen wrote in 1851, in French, to the French historian Jules Michelet on the subject of 'The Russian People and Socialism'. In this letter Herzen tried to persuade a Western readership that the Russian peasant was instinctively socialistic.

The Russian peasant has no other morality than that which flows quite instinctively and naturally from his communal life: it is profoundly national in character and the little that he knows about the Gospels fortifies him in it: the shocking corruption of the government and of the landlords binds him ever more closely to his traditional customs and to his commune. The commune has preserved the Russian people from Mongol barbarism, from Imperial civilization, from the Europeanized landowners and from the German bureaucracy: the organic life of the commune has persisted despite all the attempts made on it by authority, badly mauled though it has been at times. By good fortune it has survived right into the period that witnesses the rise of Socialism in Europe.

For Russia this has been a most happy providence.

From Alexander Herzen, 'The Russian People and Socialism', translated by Richard Wollheim, [13], pp. 184–6.

DOCUMENT 10   A SLAVOPHILE VIEW OF THE RUSSIAN
               PEOPLE

In a memorandum written in 1855 to the new tsar, Konstantin Aksakov expresses the Slavophiles' conception of the non-political nature of the Russian common people and the consequent legitimacy and necessity of autocracy as Russia's form of government.

It is difficult to understand Russia unless one can rid oneself of Western concepts, on the basis of which we expect to see in every country – and therefore in Russia too – either revolutionary or conservative elements. Both are alien to us; they are opposite extremes of the political spirit; neither is present in the Russian people, for the Russian people do not possess a political spirit ... Only monarchical power is absolute. Only under absolute monarchical authority can the people distance themselves from the state and avoid all participation in government and all political significance, thus reserving for themselves a communal moral life and the pursuit of spiritual freedom. Precisely such a monarchical government was chosen by the Russian people. This attitude on the part of the Russian is the attitude of a *free* man. By recognising the absolute authority of the state he retains his complete independence of spirit, conscience and thought. In his awareness of this moral freedom within himself the Russian is in truth not a slave, but a free man. For the Russian, absolute monarchical government is not an enemy, not something to be opposed, but a friend and defender of freedom – of that true, spiritual freedom which manifests itself in openly expressed opinion. Only when they possess such total freedom can the people be of use to the government. Political freedom is not freedom. Only when the people are completely separated from state power, only under an absolute monarchy which affords the people the full possibility of leading their spiritual life to the full, can true freedom exist on earth. This is the kind of freedom granted us by our Saviour in the words: 'Wherever there is the spirit of the Lord, there is freedom'.

From Leatherbarrow and Offord, [20], pp. 86, 99–100.

DOCUMENT 11   A SLAVOPHILE VIEW OF ORTHODOXY

In this epistle to the Serbs, written by Khomiakov in 1860 and co-signed by other Slavophiles, Khomiakov underlines the differences, as Slavophiles see them, between Orthodoxy and Catholicism.

It is no accident that the commune, the sanctity of the communal verdict and the unquestioning submission of each individual to the unanimous decision of his brethren are preserved only in Orthodox countries. The teachings of the faith cultivate the soul even in social life. The Papist seeks extraneous and personal authority, just as he is used to submitting to such authority in matters of faith; the Protestant takes personal freedom to the extreme of blind arrogance, just as in his sham worship. Such is the spirit of their teaching. Only the Orthodox Christian, preserving his freedom, yet humbly acknowledging his weakness, subordinates his freedom to the unanimous resolution of the collective conscience.

From Leatherbarrow and Offord, [20], p. 94.

DOCUMENT 12   THE RADICAL VIEW OF LIBERALISM

In this extract from his article of 1858 on 'The Struggle of Parties in France under Louis XVIII and Charles X', Chernyshevsky argues that the freedom prized by liberals is of a very limited character and that the rights they advocate are of little practical significance.

Thus liberals are almost always opposed to democrats and are hardly ever radicals.

They desire political freedom, but since political freedom almost always suffers when great upheavals take place in civil society, even freedom itself, the highest goal of all their aspirations, they wish to introduce gradually and to extend little by little without, as far as possible, any tremors. Freedom of the printed word and the existence of parliamentary government seem to them a necessary condition of political freedom; but since freedom of speech, given the present condition of Western European societies, generally becomes a vehicle for democratic, impassioned and radical propaganda, they wish to keep freedom of speech within fairly narrow boundaries lest it should turn against them. Parliamentary debates are also bound everywhere to take on a radical-democratic character if parliament is to consist of representatives of the nation in the broad sense of the word, and so liberals are compelled also to restrict participation in parliament to those classes of the people who are quite well off or even very well off under the present Western European social orders.

From a theoretical point of view liberalism may seem attractive to a person spared by good fortune from material need: freedom is a very pleasant thing. But liberalism conceives freedom in a very narrow, purely formal way. It sees freedom as an abstract right, as permission on paper, as the absence of legal prohibition. It will not understand that legal permission only has any value for a man when he has the material means to take advantage of this permission. Neither you nor I, reader, is forbidden to dine off a golden dinner service; unfortunately neither you nor I has or, in all probability, ever will have the means with which to put this refined idea into practice; for this reason I say frankly that I place no value whatever on my right to have a golden dinner service and am ready to sell this right for a silver ruble or even less. All those rights for which liberals plead are exactly like that for the common people. The people are ignorant and in almost all countries the majority of them are illiterate; having no money with which to obtain an education, having no money with which to give their children an education, how are they to value their right of free speech? Need and ignorance deprive the people of any opportunity to understand the affairs of state and to devote themselves to them – so tell me now, will the people place any value on the right to hold parliamentary debates, and will they be able to make use of it?

From Leatherbarrow and Offord, [20], pp. 204–5.

DOCUMENT 13   CHERNYSHEVSKY: 'THE ANTHROPOLOGICAL
PRINCIPLE IN PHILOSOPHY'

*In these extracts from a major article of 1860, Chernyshevsky hopes to use
the method of the natural sciences to argue the case for materialism, determinism and utilitarianism. He contends that humans possess no spiritual
dimension, have no independent will and are motivated exclusively by self-
interest and that the greatest good is the good of the greatest number.*

The natural sciences serve as a basis for that part of philosophy which examines questions concerning man just as they do for the other part which examines questions concerning external Nature. The idea, formulated by the
natural sciences, of the unity of the human organism serves as a principle of
the philosophical view of human life and all its phenomena; the observations
of physiologists, zoologists and physicians have removed any idea of dualism
in man. Philosophy sees in man what medicine, physiology and chemistry see
in him; these sciences demonstrate that no dualism is apparent in man and
philosophy adds that if man did have another nature, besides his real one,
then this other nature would necessarily reveal itself in some way, and since it
does not reveal itself in any way, since everything that occurs and manifests
itself in man occurs in accordance with his real nature alone, he has no other
nature ...

The first effect of the entry of the moral sciences into the field of the exact
sciences was the strict differentiation of what we know from what we do not
know ... We know positively, for example, that all phenomena of the moral
world derive one from another and from external circumstances in accordance with a law of causality and on these grounds every assumption about the
emergence of any phenomenon that is not the product of previous phenomena and external circumstances has been accepted as false. Current psychology therefore does not allow, for example, of such assumptions as: 'a man
acted badly in a given instance because he wanted to act badly and acted well
in another instance because he wanted to act well'. It says that a bad act or a
good act was necessarily the product of some moral or material fact or combination of facts, and 'wanting' here was only a subjective impression, which
attends the emergence in our consciousness of thoughts or acts out of previous thoughts, acts or external facts ... The phenomenon which we call the
will is itself a link in a series of phenomena and facts linked by a causal connection ...

... Man likes what is pleasant and does not like what is unpleasant – this
does not seem open to question, because the subject is simply repeated here in
the predicate. A is A, what is pleasant for man is pleasant for man, what is
unpleasant for man is unpleasant for man. Good is he who does good for others,
bad is he who does harm to others – this seems to be simple and clear as well.
Let us now join together these simple truths and we shall get the conclusion: a
man is good when in order to gain pleasure for himself he has to do what is

pleasant for others; he is bad when he is forced to derive his pleasure from the infliction of what is unpleasant on others. Human nature should not be taken to task here for one thing or extolled for the other; everything depends on circumstances, relations, institutions [the last word was deleted by the censor] ... If one carefully examines the motives which guide people it turns out that all deeds, good and bad, noble and base, heroic and pusillanimous, stem in all people from one source: man acts as it is most pleasant for him to act, is guided by calculation which dictates the renunciation of the lesser advantage or the lesser pleasure so that he may obtain the greater advantage, the greater pleasure ...

... It is those deeds of other people's which are useful to an individual that he calls good acts; in the view of society it is that which is useful for society as a whole or for a majority of its members that is taken to be good; finally, it is that which is useful for man in general that people in general, irrespective of nation or estate, call good. Cases in which the interests of different nations and estates are contrary to one another or to the general interests of mankind are very common; and just as common are cases in which the interests of some individual estate are contrary to the national interest ... To decide who has theoretical justice on their side in such cases is not at all difficult: the interest of mankind in general stands above the interests of an individual nation, the general interest of a whole nation stands above the interests of an individual estate, the interest of a numerous estate is above the interests of a numerically small one. In theory this gradation is beyond any doubt, it is merely an application of geometrical axioms – 'the whole is greater than a part of it', 'the greater quantity is larger than the smaller quantity' – to social problems.

From Leatherbarrow and Offord, [20], pp. 213–17, 220–22.

DOCUMENT 14   RADICAL CRITICISM AFTER THE
                CRIMEAN WAR

These extracts from Dobroliubov's famous review of Goncharov's novel, 'Oblomov', illustrate his use of works of imaginative literature as a starting point for social commentary and his anticipation of the imminent demise of the lethargic 'superfluous man' in art and society.

Goncharov would seem not to have chosen to depict a very broad area. The story of how the good-natured idler Oblomov lies around and sleeps and how neither friendship nor love can rouse him and get him to his feet is hardly a very momentous one. But Russian life finds reflection in it, before us stands a living, contemporary Russian type chiseled with ruthless rigour and accuracy; a new word in the development of our society is spoken in it and it is uttered clearly and firmly, without despair or the sanguine expectations of a child, but in full awareness of the truth. This word is *oblomovshchina* [i.e. the

Oblomov syndrome]; it provides a key to many of the riddles of Russian life and it lends Goncharov's novel far more social significance than all our accusatory novellas possess.

In the type of Oblomov and in all this *oblomovshchina* we see something more than just the felicitous creation of a powerful talent; we find in it a product of Russian life, a sign of the times ... Indeed how one senses the breath of a new life when one thinks, after reading Oblomov, what has brought this new type into being in literature. One cannot attribute this just to the personal talent of the author and to the breadth of his outlook. We find both a powerful talent and the broadest and most humane outlook in those authors too who created the earlier types [of 'superfluous men'] which we have mentioned above. But the fact of the matter is that from the time when the first of them, Onegin [a character of Pushkin's], appeared to the present some thirty years have elapsed. What was then in embryo, what found expression only in an obscure whispered hint, has by now assumed a definite and solid form, and has been voiced openly and loudly. Words have lost their importance; society itself feels the need for real deeds.

From Leatherbarrow and Offord, [20], pp. 230–31.

DOCUMENT 15   THE PROCLAMATION 'YOUNG RUSSIA'

This extract from a proclamation written in 1862 shows the impatience of the young generation, after the emancipation of the serfs, with further advocacy of peaceful change through reform. The proclamation, which is hostile to Herzen, also sets a tone for revolutionary groups to follow.

There is only one way out of [the] terrible, oppressive situation which is ruining people nowadays and which they are wasting their best forces fighting against: a revolution, a bloody and implacable revolution, a revolution which must fundamentally change everything, everything without exception, the bases of modern society and destroy the supporters of the current order of things.

We are not frightened of it although we do know that a river of blood will flow and that innocent victims may die; we foresee all this but nevertheless welcome its onset and are ready personally to sacrifice our heads if only it would come any sooner, the long awaited [revolution]!

... We have studied the history of the West and this study has not been in vain: we shall be more consistent not only than the pitiable revolutionaries of [18]48 but even the great terrorists of [17]92, we shall not flinch if we see that in order to overthrow the contemporary order three times more blood has to be shed than was shed by the Jacobins in the [17]90s! ...

Soon, soon the day will come when we shall unfurl the great banner of the future, a red banner, and with a loud cry [shout]: 'Long live the Russian social and democratic republic!' We shall move on the Winter Palace [i.e. the residence of the royal family in St Petersburg] to destroy those who live there ...

Translated by Derek Offord from the proclamation 'Young Russia' printed in Mikh. Lemke, *Politicheskie protsessy v Rossii 1860-kh gg.*, 2nd edn, State Publishing House, Moscow-Petrograd, 1923; reprinted by Mouton, The Hague, 1968, pp. 510, 513, 518.

DOCUMENT 16   THE 'CATECHISM OF A REVOLUTIONARY'

In these extracts from the notorious 'Catechism of a Revolutionary', which was written in 1868 by Nechaev, probably in collaboration with Bakunin, the subjects of the character of the revolutionary and his relations with the society around him are broached.

1. The revolutionary is a doomed man. He has neither his own interests, nor affairs, nor feelings, nor attachments, nor property, nor even name. Everything in him is absorbed by a single, exclusive interest, by a total concept, a total passion – revolution.

2. In the depths of his being not only in words but in action he has sundered any connection with the civil order and with the entire educated world and with all the laws, proprieties, conventions, and morality of this world. He is its merciless enemy, and if he continues to live in it, then it is only in order the more certainly to destroy it ...

13. The revolutionary enters into the official world, the world of estate rankings, and the so-called educated world and lives in it only with the aim of destroying it more completely and sooner. He is not a revolutionary if he pities anything in this world, if he can hold back before the annihilation of a position, a relationship, or some person belonging to this world, in which everyone and everything must be equally despicable to him. All the worse for him if he has in it family, friendly, or love relationships; he is not a revolutionary if they can stay his hand.

14. With the goal of merciless destruction the revolutionary can and frequently even must live in society, pretending to be something other than what he is. The revolutionary must penetrate everywhere, into all strata – upper and middle, into the merchant's shop, into the church, into the manor house, into the bureaucratic, military, and literary worlds, into the Third Section, and even into the Winter Palace.

Translation by Philip Pomper, printed in his book *Sergei Nechaev*, [128], pp. 90, 92.

DOCUMENT 17   THE DEBT OF THE INTELLIGENTSIA TO
THE PEOPLE

*This is an extract from the fourth of Lavrov's 'Historical Letters' (1868–69).
Entitled 'The Price of Progress', the letter puts forward an influential formu-
lation of the obligation of members of the intelligentsia to dedicate themselves
to promotion of social justice.*

A member of that small group among the minority who see their pleasure in
their own cultivation, in seeking out truth and implementing justice, would
say to himself: 'Each comfort which I enjoy, each idea which I have had the
leisure to acquire or formulate has been bought with the blood, sufferings or
toil of millions. The past I cannot rectify, and however dearly my cultivation
might have been bought I cannot renounce it: it is the very ideal that prompts
me to act. Only an ineffectual and undeveloped person is crushed under the
responsibility which lies upon him and flees from evil to the Thebaids [mem-
bers of a monastic community in Egypt; i.e. people who seek refuge from the
world] or to the grave. Evil must be remedied as far as possible, but this may
be done only in life. One must *redeem* evil by one's deeds in life. I shall
absolve myself from responsibility for the bloody price of my cultivation if I
use this very cultivation to reduce evil in the present and the future. If I am a
cultivated person, then I am *obliged* to do this and this obligation is not at all
onerous for me, since it coincides with what I find pleasurable; by seeking and
spreading more truths, clarifying my ideas about the most just social order
and striving to put it into effect, I am increasing my own pleasure and at the
same time doing everything I can for the suffering majority in the present and
the future. And so my job is defined by one simple rule: live in accordance
with the ideal which you have set yourself, as the ideal of a *cultivated* man!'

From Leatherbarrow and Offord, [20], pp. 267–8.

DOCUMENT 18   LAVROV'S REVOLUTIONARY STRATEGY

*These extracts from the programme of the journal 'Forward!', written in
1873, show Lavrov's aversion to the concept of political revolution from
above.*

Paramount for us is the premise that the reconstruction of Russian society
must be carried out not only with the welfare of the people *as its objective,*
not only *for the benefit* of the people, but also *by* the people. The contemporary Russian activist must, in our opinion, abandon the obsolete view that revolutionary ideas formulated by a small section of the more highly developed
minority may be imposed on the people, that socialist revolutionaries, having
successfully overthrown the central government, may take its place and intro-

duce a new order by means of legislation, thus conferring benefits on the unprepared mass. We do not want any new coercive authority to take the place of the old, whatever the source of the new authority might be ... It is the responsibility of this section of the civilized Russian minority not to impose its own ideas on the people, with a view to conferring benefits on the majority, but to explain to the people their true needs and the best ways of satisfying these needs and to point out to them the force which resides in them ...

From Leatherbarrow and Offord, [20], p. 269.

DOCUMENT 19   **BAKUNIN'S REVOLUTIONARY STRATEGY**

In his so-called 'Appendix A' to 'Statism and Anarchy' (1873), Bakunin discusses the aspects of the socialist ideal supposedly alive among the peasantry, the factors that hinder its realization, and the courses open to the revolutionary intelligentsia.

Does any such ideal exist in the mentality of the Russian people? There is no doubt that it does exist and one does not even need to delve too far into the historical consciousness of our people in order to define its main features.

The first and main feature is the conviction which is universal among the people, that the land, all the land, belongs to the people who water it with their sweat and make it productive with the labour of their own hands. The second, and equally important, feature is that the right to the utilization of the land belongs not to the individual but to the whole commune, the *mir*, which periodically divides it up among individuals; the third feature, of equal importance to the two preceding ones, is a quasi-absolute autonomy, communal self-government, and, as a result of this, the thoroughly hostile attitude of the commune towards the state.

... However, the Russian popular ideal is obscured by three other features which distort its character and very greatly hamper and slow down its realization; features which we must therefore fight against with all our strength, and against which struggle is the more possible for the fact that it is already being waged among the people themselves.

These three obscuring features are: 1) the patriarchal quality of Russian life; 2) the absorption of the individual by the *mir*; 3) faith in the tsar ...

The state has utterly crushed and corrupted the Russian commune which had in any case already been corrupted by its own patriarchal principle. Under the oppression of the state even communal voting has become a fraud and the persons temporarily elected by the people themselves, headmen, elders, peasant police, foremen, have been turned into tools of authority on the one hand and suborned servants of the *kulaks* on the other. In such conditions the last vestiges of justice, truth and simple love of one's fellow humanbeings were bound to disappear from the communes, which had in any case been ruined by state taxes and obligations and squeezed to the limit by the arbitrary behaviour of the authorities. Brigandage has more than ever before become the only outlet left to an individual, and a general revolt, revolution, the only outlet left to the people as a whole.

What can our intellectual proletariat, the honest, sincere, totally committed, social-revolutionary Russian youth do in this sort of situation? It must go to the people, undoubtedly, because nowadays it is everywhere the case, and especially in Russia, that there is no longer life, or any cause or future outside the people, outside the multi-million masses, of unskilled labourers. But how and for what purpose should one go to the people?

At the present time, following the unhappy outcome of the Nechaev venture, opinions among us on this score seem to be sharply divided; but out of the general mess of ideas two principal and opposite tendencies already stand out. One is of a more pacific and preparatory nature; the other is rebellious and aspires directly to the organization of a force for the people's defence ...

... It is in this [latter] way that we believe and it is only from this way that we expect salvation.

Our people plainly need help. They are in such a desperate position that one could raise up any village with no trouble at all. But although any uprising, however unsuccessful, is always useful, nevertheless individual eruptions are not enough. All the villages must be raised up at once. That this is possible is proved by the huge popular movements led by Stenka Razin and Pugachov.

From Leatherbarrow and Offord, [20], pp. 278–9, 282–4.

DOCUMENT 20   TKACHOV'S REVOLUTIONARY STRATEGY

These extracts from the programme of the journal 'The Tocsin', written in 1875, underline Tkachov's conception of the urgency and nature of the revolutionary coup d'état which he recommends.

Today our state is a fiction, a legend which has no roots in the people's life. It is odious to all; in all, even its own servants, it inspires blind malice and servile fear mixed with the lackey's scorn. People are afraid of it because it possesses material strength; but once it loses this strength not a single hand will be raised in its defence.

But tomorrow all today's enemies will stand up for it, tomorrow it will express their interests, the interests of the *kulaks* and bloodsuckers, the interests of private property, the interests of trade and industry, the interests of the bourgeois world which is coming into being.

Today it is absolutely absurd and absurdly absolute.

Tomorrow it will become constitutional and modern, thrifty and prudent. So hurry!

Sound the Tocsin! Sound the Tocsin! ...

... the immediate aim of the revolution must be the seizure of political power, the creation of a revolutionary state. But the seizure of power, while it is a necessary condition of the revolution, is still not the revolution. It is only its prelude. The revolution is effected by the revolutionary state which, on the one hand, struggles with and destroys the conservative and reactionary elements of society, and abolishes all those institutions which impede the establishment of equality and brotherhood, and, on the other hand, brings into being institutions which promote their development.

Thus the activity of the revolutionary state must be twofold: revolutionary-destructive and revolutionary-constructive ...

If the revolutionaries' short-term task, which may in practice be accomplished, amounts to a violent attack on the existing political power with the purpose of seizing this power into their own hands, then it follows that all the efforts of a truly revolutionary party must be directed to the fulfilment of precisely this task. It is easiest and most convenient to fulfil it by means of a state conspiracy. Thus a state conspiracy is, if not the sole means, then at any rate the main and most expedient means of carrying out violent revolution. But anyone who acknowledges the need for a state conspiracy must by the same token acknowledge too the need for a disciplined organization of revolutionary forces.

From Leatherbarrow and Offord, [20], pp. 288, 291–2.

DOCUMENT 21   **THE DEMANDS OF THE PEOPLE'S WILL**

On 10 March 1881, just over a week after the assassination of Alexander II, the Executive Committee of The People's Will addressed a letter to the new tsar arguing that a continuation of the revolutionary struggle was inevitable unless power was transferred to the people. This extract summarizes their demands.

The conditions necessary if the revolutionary movement is to be replaced by peaceful work have been created by history, not by us. We do not lay them down but merely remind you of them.

There are in our view two of these conditions:

1) A general amnesty for all political crimes committed in the past, since these were not crimes but the fulfilment of civic duty.

2) The convocation of representatives from the whole Russian people to review the existing forms of state and social life and remould them in conformity with the wishes of the people.

It is however incumbent upon us to note that the legitimation of supreme power by popular representation may only be achieved if elections are conducted completely freely. Therefore elections must be conducted in the following conditions:

1) Deputies are to be sent by all classes and estates [i.e. classes] without distinction and in proportion to the number of inhabitants [in that class or estate];

2) there must be no restrictions on either electors or deputies;
3) electoral agitation and the elections themselves must be conducted completely freely and the government must therefore allow, as a temporary measure pending the decision of a popular assembly: a) complete freedom of press; b) complete freedom of speech; c) complete freedom of assembly; d) complete freedom of electoral programmes.

Translated by Derek Offord from Vera Figner, *Zapechatlionnyi trud*, Mysl′, Moscow 1964, vol. ii, p. 411.

DOCUMENT 22   **PREFACE TO THE 1882 RUSSIAN EDITION OF THE 'MANIFESTO OF THE COMMUNIST PARTY'**

In their preface to the second Russian edition of The Communist Manifesto, *Marx and Engels, to the consternation of the first Russian Marxist group, allow of the possibility that Russia might reach socialism by a route different from that prescribed by them for Western European countries.*

The Communist Manifesto had as its object the proclamation of the inevitably impending dissolution of modern bourgeois property. But in Russia we find, face to face with the rapidly developing capitalist swindle and bourgeois landed property, just beginning to develop, more than half the land owned in common by the peasants. Now the question is: can the Russian *obshchina*, though greatly undermined, yet a form of the primeval common ownership of land, pass directly to the higher form of communist common ownership? Or, on the contrary, must it first pass through the same process of dissolution as constitutes the historical evolution of the West? The only answer to that possible today is this: if the Russian Revolution becomes the signal for a proletarian revolution in the West, so that both complement each other, the present Russian common ownership of land may serve as the starting point for a communist development.

From Karl Marx and Friedrich Engels, *Manifesto of the Communist Party*.

DOCUMENT 23   **TOLSTOY'S ANARCHIST PACIFISM**

These brief extracts from one of Tolstoy's late treatises illustrate Tolstoy's abhorrence of the coercion on which political power rests.

All men of the modern world exist in a continual and flagrant antagonism which is expressed in economic as well as in political relations. But most striking of all is the contradiction between the Christian law of the brotherhood of man, which exists in men's consciousness, and the necessity (under which the general law of compulsory military service places everyone) of each of them being ready for enmity and murder – each of them being at one and the same time a Christian and a gladiator ...

The basis of power is physical violence. And the possibility of inflicting physical violence on people is afforded chiefly by an organization of armed men trained to act in unison in submission to one will. Such bands of armed men submissive to a single will are what constitute an army. An army has always been and still is the basis of power ...

Governments assert that armies are needed first of all against their own subjects, and every man who performs military service involuntarily becomes an accomplice in all the acts of violence the government inflicts on its subjects.

From Tolstoy, *The Kingdom of God is within You*, [29], pp. 158–9, 199–200, 212.

DOCUMENT 24   A MARXIST VIEW OF CAPITALISM IN RUSSIA

In his work 'Our Differences', published in 1885, Plekhanov contended that capitalism was inexorably developing in Russia. In these extracts from the end of chapter 3 of this work he summarizes the conclusion to which his investigation of the internal market, the number of workers, the state of cottage industry and factory industry, the decay of the peasant commune and other economic factors has led him.

All the latest, and therefore most influential currents in our social life, all the most significant facts in the sphere of production and exchange, have one unquestionable, incontrovertible meaning: they are not only clearing the road for capitalism, they are also themselves factors that are necessary and important in the highest degree in capitalism's development. *In favour of capitalism* are the whole dynamic of our social life, all the forces which develop as the social mechanism moves and which in turn determine the direction and speed of the mechanism's movement. *Against capitalism* stand only the more or less debatable interests of a section of the peasantry together with the force of inertia which at times so painfully makes itself felt among cultivated people in any backward agricultural country ... The main stream of Russian capitalism is not yet large; there are as yet not many places in Russia where relations between the man hiring labour and the worker entirely correspond to the commonplace notion of the relations between labour and capital in capitalist society; but such a multitude of large and small brooks, streams and rivers is flowing into that current from all sides that the total mass of water flowing towards it is enormous and the rapid and intense growth of the current is not open to question. It can no longer be stopped, still less can it be dried up; it remains only to regulate its flow if we do not want it to bring us only harm and if we are not to abandon hope of at least partially subjugating the elemental force of nature to the rational activity of man.

Translated by Derek Offord from G. V. Plekhanov, *Sochineniia*, 3rd edn, State Publishing House, Moscow/Leningrad, 1923–27, vol. ii, pp. 270–71.

BIBLIOGRAPHY

For the convenience of the reader the secondary sources listed in this bibliography are divided into categories, but these categories should not be regarded as rigid. The boundary between radical thought and the revolutionary movement in particular is unclear and some works (e.g. nos 123, 129) might be placed with equal justification in either category.

Only secondary sources written in or translated into English are given here. There is of course a huge secondary literature, as well as primary sources, in Russian.

Also omitted, but essential to a full understanding of Russian history of the late imperial period, are the major works of fiction by classical authors such as Chekhov, Dostoevsky, Gogol, Goncharov, Lermontov, Ostrovsky, Pushkin, Tolstoy and Turgenev.

The place of publication of works published by Cambridge University Press or by Oxford University Press is not given. The place of publication of other works cited here is London unless otherwise stated.

PRIMARY SOURCES

Translations of works of Russian thought, memoirs and documents

1   Annenkov, P. V., *The Extraordinary Decade: Literary Memoirs* , tr. Irwin R. Titunik, ed. Arthur P. Mendel, Ardis, Ann Arbor, Michigan, 1968.

2   Bakunin, M. A., *Selected Writings*, tr. Steven Cox and Olive Stevens, ed. and introduced by Arthur Lehning, Jonathan Cape, 1973.

3   Bakunin, M. A., *Statism and Anarchy*, tr. and ed. Marshall S. Shatz, Cambridge University Press, 1990.

4   Belinsky, V. G., *Selected Philosophical Works*, Hyperion Press, Westport, Connecticut, 1981; reprint of edn by Foreign Languages Publishing House, Moscow, 1956.

5   Chaadaev, P. Ia., *Philosophical Letters and Apology of a Madman*, tr. with an introduction by Mary–Barbara Zeldin, University of Tennessee, Knoxville, Tennessee, 1969.

6   Chernyshevsky, N. G., *Selected Philosophical Essays*, Hyperion Press, Westport, Connecticut, 1981; reprint of edn by Foreign Languages Publishing House, Moscow, 1953.

7   Chernyshevsky, N. G., *What is to be done?*, tr. Benjamin R. Tucker, expanded by Cathy Porter, Virago Press, 1982; also tr. Michael R. Katz, annotated by William G. Wagner, Cornell University Press, Ithaca, New York State, 1989.

8   Custine, The Marquis de, *Russia*, tr. and abridged from the French, Longman, Brown, Green, and Longmans, 1854; an acerbic view of the country by an aristocratic French traveller.

9   Dobroliubov, N. A., *Selected Philosophical Essays*, tr. J. Fineberg, Hyperion Press, Westport, Connecticut, 1983; reprint of edn by Foreign Languages Publishing House, Moscow, 1948.

10 Edie, James M., James P. Scanlan and Mary–Barbara Zeldin, eds, *Russian Philosophy*, 3 vols, Quadrangle Books, Chicago, Illinois, 1965.

11 Gogol, N.V., *Selected Passages from Correspondence with Friends*, tr. Jesse Zeldin, Vanderbilt University Press, Nashville, Tennessee, 1969.

12 Haxthausen, Baron A. von, *The Russian Empire: Its People, Institutions and Resources*, 2 vols, Frank Cass, 1968; reprint of the first English edn, Chapman and Hall, 1856; German original published in 3 vols, the first two in 1847 and the third in 1852.

13 Herzen, A. I., *From the Other Shore and the Russian People and Socialism*, tr. Moura Budberg and Richard Wollheim, Weidenfeld and Nicolson, 1956.

14 Herzen, A. I., *My Past and Thoughts*, tr. Constance Garnett, revised by Humphrey Higgens, with an introduction by Isaiah Berlin, 4 vols, Chatto and Windus, 1968.

15 Herzen, A. I., *Selected Philosophical Works*, tr. L. Navrozov, Foreign Languages Publishing House, Moscow, 1956.

16 *Karamzin's Memoir on Ancient and Modern Russia: A Translation and Analysis*, by Richard Pipes, Harvard University Press, Cambridge, Massachusetts, 1959.

17 Kropotkin, Peter, *The Conquest of Bread and Other Writings*, ed. Marshall Shatz, Cambridge University Press, 1995.

18 Kropotkin, Peter, *Memoirs of a Revolutionist*, 2 vols, Smith, Elder, 1899.

19 Lavrov, P. L., *Historical Letters*, tr. James P. Scanlan, University of California Press, Berkeley and Los Angeles, 1967.

20 Leatherbarrow, W. J., and D. C. Offord, eds, *A Documentary History of Russian Thought from the Enlightenment to Marxism*, Ardis, Ann Arbor, Michigan, 1987.

21   Lenin [V. I. Ulianov], *What is to be done?*, tr. S. V. and Patricia
      Utechin, ed. with an introduction and notes by S. V. Utechin, Claren-
      don Press, Oxford, 1963; also tr. Joe Fineberg and George Hanna;
      revisions to translation, and introduction and glossary by Robert
      Service, Penguin, Harmondsworth, 1988.
22   Matlaw, Ralph E., ed., *Belinsky, Chernyshevsky, and Dobrolyubov:
      Selected Criticism*, Indiana University Press, Bloomington, Indiana,
      1976; originally published by Dutton, New York, 1962.
23   Pisarev, D. I., *Selected Philosophical, Social and Political Essays*,
      Foreign Languages Publishing House, Moscow, 1958.
24   Plekhanov, G. V., *Selected Philosophical Works*, 5 vols; vol. i published
      by Lawrence and Wishart, London, 1961; vols ii–v published by
      Progress Publishers, Moscow, 1976–81.
25   Radishchev, A. N., *A Journey from St. Petersburg to Moscow*, tr. Leo
      Wiener, ed. with an introduction and notes by Roderick Page Thaler,
      Harvard University Press, Cambridge, Massachusetts, 1958; 3rd
      printing 1969.
26   Raeff, Marc, *The Decembrist Movement*, Prentice-Hall, Englewood
      Cliffs, New Jersey, 1966; translated documents with a useful intro-
      duction.
27   Raeff, Marc, *Russian Intellectual History: An Anthology*, Harcourt
      Brace and World, 1966; reprinted by Humanities Press, New Jersey/
      Harvester Press, Sussex, 1978.
28   Tolstoy, L. N., *A Confession and Other Religious Writings*, tr. and
      with an introduction by Jane Kentish, Penguin, Harmondsworth,
      1987.
29   Tolstoy, L. N., 'The Kingdom of God is within You', in *The Kingdom
      of God and Peace Essays*, tr. and with an introduction by Aylmer
      Maude, Oxford University Press, first published 1936.
30   Tolstoy, L. N., *What is Art?*, tr. Aylmer Maude, ed. with an introduc-
      tion and notes by W. Gareth Jones, Bristol Classical Press/
      Duckworth, 1994.
31   Vernadsky, George, *et al.*, eds, *A Source Book for Russian History
      from Early Times to 1917*, Yale University Press, New Haven, Con-
      necticut, 1972, vols ii–iii.

SECONDARY SOURCES

Historical background

32   Anisimov, Evgenii V., *The Reforms of Peter the Great: Progress
      through Coercion in Russia*, tr. with an introduction by John T.
      Alexander, M. E. Sharpe, Armonk, New York, 1993.
33   Blum, Jerome, *Lord and Peasant in Russia: From the Ninth to the
      Nineteenth Century*, Princeton University Press, Princeton, New
      Jersey, 1961.

34   Florinsky, M. T., *Russia: A History and an Interpretation*, 2 vols, Macmillan, New York, 1947 and 1953.
35   Gershenkron, A., 'Agrarian policies and industrialization: Russia 1861–1917', in *The Cambridge Economic History*, vol. vi, part 1, Cambridge University Press, 1966.
36   Lincoln, W. Bruce, *The Great Reforms: Autocracy, Bureaucracy, and the Politics of Change in Imperial Russia*, Northern Illinois University Press, DeKalb, Illinois, 1990.
37   Lincoln, W. Bruce, *Nicholas I: Emperor and Autocrat of All the Russias*, Allen Lane, 1978.
38   Mosse, Werner E., *Alexander II and the Modernization of Russia*, I. B. Tauris, 1992; originally published by The English Universities Press, 1958.
39   Pipes, Richard, *Russia under the Old Regime*, Penguin, Harmondsworth, 1977.
40   Portal, Roger, 'The industrialization of Russia', in *The Cambridge Economic History*, vol. vi, part 1, Cambridge University Press, 1966.
41   Raeff, Marc, *Michael Speransky: Statesman of Imperial Russia, 1772–1839*, Martinus Nijhoff, The Hague, 1957.
42   Raeff, Marc, *Origins of the Russian Intelligentsia: The Eighteenth-Century Nobility*, Harcourt, Brace and World, New York, 1966.
43   Riasanovsky, Nicholas V., *A History of Russia* (part 5), 5th edn, Oxford University Press, 1993.
44   Saunders, David, *Russia in the Age of Reaction and Reform, 1801–1881*, Longman, 1992.
45   Seton–Watson, H., *The Russian Empire, 1801–1917*, Clarendon Press, Oxford, 1967.
46   Squire, P.S., *The Third Department: The Establishment and Practices of the Political Police in the Russia of Nicholas I*, Cambridge University Press, 1968.
47   Sumner, B. H., *Peter the Great and the Emergence of Russia*, English Universities Press, 1972; reprint of 1951 edn.
48   Vernadsky, G., *A History of Russia* (chapter 7 on), 5th revised edn, Yale University Press, New Haven, Connecticut, 1961.

Cultural background

49   Confino, Michael, 'On intellectuals and intellectual traditions in eighteenth- and nineteenth–century Russia', *Daedalus*, vol. ci, no. 2, Spring 1972.
50   Cornwell, Neil, ed., *Reference Guide to Russian Literature*, Fitzroy Dearborn, 1998.
51   Freeborn, Richard, *The Rise of the Russian Novel: Studies in the Russian Novel from 'Eugene Onegin' to 'War and Peace'*, Cambridge University Press, 1973.
52   Freeborn, Richard, *The Russian Revolutionary Novel: Turgenev to Pasternak*, Cambridge University Press, 1982.

53   Malia, Martin, 'What is the intelligentsia?', in Richard Pipes, ed., *The Russian Intelligentsia*, Columbia University Press, New York, 1961.

54   Martinsen, Deborah A., *Literary Journals in Imperial Russia*, Cambridge University Press, 1997.

55   Mathewson, Rufus W., Jr, *The Positive Hero in Russian Literature*, Columbia University Press, New York, 1958; revised edn, Stanford University Press, Stanford, California, 1975.

56   Mirsky, D. S., *A History of Russian Literature*, ed. and abridged by Francis J. Whitfield, Alfred A. Knopf, New York, 1949/Routledge and Kegan Paul, 1949.

57   Monas, Sidney, *The Third Section: Police and Society under Nicholas I*, Harvard University Press, Cambridge, Massachusetts, 1961.

58   Moser, Charles A., ed., *The Cambridge History of Russian Literature*, Cambridge University Press, 1989; revised edn 1992.

59   Riasanovsky, Nicholas V., *The Image of Peter the Great in Russian History and Thought*, Oxford University Press, 1985.

60   Riasanovsky, Nicholas V., *Nicholas I and Official Nationality in Russia, 1825–1855*, University of California Press, Berkeley and Los Angeles, 1959.

61   Riasanovsky, Nicholas V., *A Parting of Ways: Government and the Educated Public in Russia, 1801–1855*, Clarendon Press, Oxford, 1976.

62   Schapiro, Leonard, *Turgenev: His Life and Times*, Oxford University Press, 1978.

63   Terras, Victor, ed., *Handbook of Russian Literature*, Yale University Press, New Haven, Connecticut, 1985.

64   Terras, Victor, *A History of Russian Literature*, Yale University Press, New Haven, Connecticut, 1991.

65   Ware, Timothy, *The Orthodox Church*, Penguin, Harmondsworth, 1963.

General works on Russian thought

66   Berdiaev, Nicolas, *The Origin of Russian Communism*, tr. R. M. French, Geoffrey Bles, 1948.

67   Berdiaev, Nicolas, *The Russian Idea*, tr. R. M. French, Geoffrey Bles, 1947; originally published by YMCA Press, Paris, 1946.

68   Berlin, Isaiah, *Russian Thinkers*, ed. Henry Hardy and Aileen Kelly, Hogarth Press, 1978.

69   Copleston, Frederick C., *Philosophy in Russia: From Herzen to Lenin and Berdyaev*, Search Press, Tunbridge Wells/University of Notre Dame Press, Notre Dame, Indiana, 1986.

70   Lossky, N. O., *History of Russian Philosophy*, Allen and Unwin, 1952.

71   Masaryk, Thomas Garrigue, *The Spirit of Russia: Studies in Literature, History and Philosophy*, vols i–ii, tr. Eden and Cedar Paul, George Allen and Unwin, 1919; vol. iii, ed. George Gibian, tr. Robert Bass, George Allen and Unwin, 1967.

72 Schapiro, Leonard, *Rationalism and Nationalism in Russian Nine-teenth-Century Political Thought*, Yale University Press, New Haven, Connecticut, 1967.

73 Schapiro, Leonard, *Russian Studies*, ed. Ellen Dahrendorf and with an introduction by Harry Willetts, Collins Harvill, 1986.

74 Utechin, S. V., *Russian Political Thought: A Concise History*, J. M. Dent and Sons, 1963.

75 Walicki, Andrzej, *A History of Russian Thought from the Enlighten-ment to Marxism*, tr. Hilda Andrews–Rusiecka, Clarendon Press, Oxford, 1980.

76 Zenkovsky, V. V., *A History of Russian Philosophy*, 2 vols, tr. George L. Kline, Routledge and Kegan Paul, 1953.

Decembrism

77 Mazour, Anatole G., *The First Russian Revolution, 1825: The Decem-brist Movement, Its Origins, Development and Significance* , Stanford University Press, Stanford, California, 1937; reprinted 1961; a thorough survey but with a perhaps unduly sympathetic treatment of Pestel.

78 O'Meara, Patrick, *K. F. Ryleev: A Political Biography of the Decem-brist Poet*, Princeton University Press, Princeton, New Jersey, 1984.

79 Zetlin, Mikhail, *The Decembrists*, tr. George Panin, International Uni-versities Press, New York, 1958.

Chaadaev

80 McNally, Raymond T., *Chaadayev and his Friends: An Intellectual History of Peter Chaadayev and His Russian Contemporaries*, Diplo-matic Press, Tallahassee, Florida, 1971.

81 McNally, Raymond T., 'Chaadaev's evaluation of Peter the Great', *Slavic Review*, vol. xxiii, no.1, March 1964.

82 McNally, Raymond T., 'Chaadayev's evaluation of Western Christian Churches', *The Slavonic and East European Review*, vol. xlii, no. 99, June 1964.

Conservative nationalist thought

83 Black, J. L., *Nicholas Karamzin and Russian Society in the Nineteenth Century: A Study in Russian Political and Historical Thought*, Uni-versity of Toronto Press, Toronto/Buffalo, 1975.

84 Christoff, Peter K., *An Introduction to Nineteenth-Century Russian Slavophilism: Iu. F. Samarin*, Westview Press, Boulder, Colorado, 1991.

85 Christoff, Peter K., *An Introduction to Nineteenth-Century Russian Slavophilism: A Study in Ideas*, vol. ii, *I. V. Kireevskij*, Mouton, The Hague, 1972.

86 Christoff, Peter K., *K. S. Aksakov: A Study in Ideas*, Princeton Univer-sity Press, Princeton, New Jersey, 1982.

87 Dowler, Wayne, *Dostoevsky, Grigor'ev, and Native Soil Conservatism*, University of Toronto Press, Toronto/Buffalo/London, 1982.

88 Dowler, Wayne, *An Unnecessary Man: The Life of Apollon Grigor'ev*, University of Toronto Press, Toronto/Buffalo/London, 1995.

89 Frank, Joseph, *Dostoevsky*, 4 vols to date, Princeton University Press, Princeton, New Jersey, 1976– .

90 Gerstein, Linda, *Nikolai Strakhov*, Harvard University Press, Cambridge, Massachusetts, 1971.

91 Gleason, Abbott, *European and Muscovite: Ivan Kireevsky and the Origins of Slavophilism*, Harvard University Press, Cambridge, Massachusetts, 1972.

92 Kochetkova, Natalya, *Nikolay Karamzin*, Twayne, Boston, Massachusetts, 1975.

93 Lukashevich, Stephen, *Ivan Aksakov, 1823–1886: A Study in Russian Thought and Politics*, Harvard University Press, Cambridge, Massachusetts, 1965.

94 MacMaster, Robert E., *Danilevsky: A Russian Totalitarian Philosopher*, Harvard University Press, Cambridge, Massachusetts, 1967.

95 Martin, Alexander, *Romantics, Reformers, Reactionaries: Russian Conservative Thought and Politics in the Reign of Alexander I*, Northern Illinois University Press, DeKalb, Illinois, 1997.

96 Peace, Richard, *Dostoyevsky: An Examination of the Major Novels*, Cambridge University Press, 1971.

97 Riasanovsky, Nicholas V., *Russia and the West in the Teaching of the Slavophiles: A Study of Romantic Ideology*, Peter Smith, Gloucester, Massachusetts, 1965.

98 Thaden, Edward C., *Conservative Nationalism in Nineteenth-Century Russia*, University of Washington Press, Seattle, Washington, 1964.

99 Walicki, Andrzej, *The Slavophile Controversy: History of a Conservative Utopia in Nineteenth-Century Russian Thought*, tr. Hilda Andrews–Rusiecka, Clarendon Press, Oxford, 1975.

Liberal thought

100 Field, Daniel, 'Kavelin and Russian liberalism', *Slavic Review*, vol. xxxii, no. 1, March 1973.

101 Fischer, George, *Russian Liberalism: From Gentry to Intelligentsia*, Harvard University Press, Cambridge, Massachusetts, 1958.

102 Hamburg, G. M., *Boris Chicherin and Early Russian Liberalism, 1828–1866*, Stanford University Press, Stanford, California, 1992.

103 Offord, Derek, *Portraits of Early Russian Liberals: A Study of the Thought of T. N. Granovsky, V. P. Botkin, P. V. Annenkov, A. V. Druzhinin, and K. D. Kavelin*, Cambridge University Press, 1985.

104 Roosevelt, Priscilla Reynolds, *Apostle of Russian Liberalism: Timofei Granovsky*, Oriental Research Partners, Newtonville, Massachusetts, 1986.

Radical thought

105 Acton, Edward, *Alexander Herzen and the Role of the Intellectual Revolutionary*, Cambridge University Press, 1979.

106 Bowman, Herbert E., *Vissarion Belinski 1811–48: A Study in the Origins of Social Criticism in Russia*, Harvard University Press, Cambridge, Massachusetts, 1954; reprinted by Russell and Russell, New York, 1969.

107 Carr, Edward Hallett, *The Romantic Exiles: A Nineteenth-Century Portrait Gallery*, Penguin, Harmondsworth, 1968; first published by Victor Gollancz, 1933.

108 Kelly, Aileen, *Mikhail Bakunin: A Study in the Psychology and Politics of Utopianism*, Clarendon Press, Oxford, 1982.

109 Lampert, Evgeny, *Sons against Fathers: Studies in Russian Radicalism and Revolution*, Clarendon Press, Oxford, 1965; on Chernyshevsky, Dobroliubov and Pisarev.

110 Lampert, Evgeny, *Studies in Rebellion*, Routledge and Kegan Paul, 1957; on Bakunin, Belinsky and Herzen.

111 Lang, David Marshall, *The First Russian Radical: Alexander Radishchev, 1749–1802*, Allen and Unwin, 1959.

112 McConnell, Allen, *A Russian Philosophe: Alexander Radishchev, 1749–1802*, Martinus Nijhoff, The Hague, 1964.

113 Malia, Martin, *Alexander Herzen and the Birth of Russian Socialism, 1812–1855*, Harvard University Press, Cambridge, Massachusetts, 1961.

114 Moser, Charles A., *Esthetics as Nightmare: Russian Literary Theory, 1855–1870*, Princeton University Press, Princeton, New Jersey, 1989.

115 Offord, Derek, 'The contribution of V. V. Bervi–Flerovsky to Russian populism', *The Slavonic and East European Review*, vol. lxvi, no. 2, April 1988.

116 Paperno, I., *Chernyshevsky and the Age of Realism: A Study in the Semiotics of Behavior*, Stanford University Press, Stanford, California, 1988.

117 Pereira, N. G. O., *The Thought and Teachings of N. G. Černyševskij*, Mouton, The Hague, 1975.

118 Randall, Francis B., *N. G. Chernyshevskii*, Twayne, New York, 1967.

119 Seddon, J. H., *The Petrashevtsy: A Study of the Russian Revolutionaries of 1848*, Manchester University Press, Manchester, 1985.

120 Terras, V., *Belinskij and Russian Literary Criticism: The Heritage of Organic Aesthetics*, University of Wisconsin Press, Madison, Wisconsin, 1974.

121 Wellek, R., 'Social and aesthetic values in Russian nineteenth-century literary criticism', in E. J. Simmons, ed., *Continuity and Change in Russian and Soviet Thought*, Harvard University Press, Cambridge, Massachusetts, 1955; reprinted by Russell and Russell, New York, 1967.

122   Woehrlin, William F., *Chernyshevskii: The Man and the Journalist*, Harvard University Press, Cambridge, Massachusetts, 1971.

The revolutionary movement up to 1881

123   Billington, James H., *Mikhailovsky and Russian Populism*, Clarendon Press, Oxford, 1958.

124   Carr, E. H., *Michael Bakunin*, Macmillan, 1937; republished by Vintage Books, New York, 1961.

125   Footman, David, *Red Prelude: A Life of A. I. Zhelyabov*, The Cresset Press, 1944; 2nd edn, 1968.

126   Hardy, Deborah, *Petr Tkachev, The Critic as Jacobin*, University of Washington Press, Seattle, Washington, 1977.

127   Pomper, Philip, *Peter Lavrov and the Russian Revolutionary Movement*, University of Chicago Press, Chicago, Illinois, 1972.

128   Pomper, Philip, *Sergei Nechaev*, Rutgers University Press, New Brunswick, New Jersey, 1979.

129   Venturi, Franco, *Roots of Revolution: A History of the Populist and Socialist Movements in Nineteenth-Century Russia*, tr. F. Haskell, Weidenfeld and Nicolson, 1960; still the definitive history of the revolutionary movement up to 1881; also useful on the radical thinkers of the 1850s and 1860s.

130   Weeks, Albert L., *The First Bolshevik: A Political Biography of Peter Tkachev*, New York University Press, New York, 1968.

131   Woodcock, George, *Anarchism: A History of Libertarian Ideas and Movements*, 2nd edn, Penguin, Harmondsworth, 1986; has chapters on Bakunin and the revolutionary movement in Russia in the 1870s; also chapters on Kropotkin and Tolstoy.

132   Yarmolinsky, A., *Road to Revolution: A Century of Russian Radicalism*, Collier Books, New York, 1962.

Opposition after 1881

133   Baron, Samuel H., *Plekhanov: The Father of Russian Marxism*, Routledge and Kegan Paul, 1963.

134   Christian, Reginald Frank, *Tolstoy: A Critical Introduction*, Cambridge University Press, 1969.

135   Gifford, Henry, *Tolstoy*, Oxford University Press, 1982; in the Past Masters series.

136   Haimson, Leopold H., *The Russian Marxists and the Origins of Bolshevism*, Harvard University Press, Cambridge, Massachusetts, 1955; republished by Beacon Press, Boston, Massachusetts, 1966.

137   Harding, Neil, *Lenin's Political Thought*, vol. i, Macmillan, 1977.

138   Keep, J. L. H., *The Rise of Social Democracy in Russia*, Clarendon Press, Oxford, 1963.

139   Kindersley, Richard, *The First Russian Revisionists: A Study of Legal Marxism in Russia*, Clarendon Press, Oxford, 1962.

140 Mendel, Arthur P., *Dilemmas of Progress in Tsarist Russia: Legal Marxism and Legal Populism*, Harvard University Press, Cambridge, Massachusetts, 1961.

141 Miller, Martin A., *Kropotkin*, University of Chicago Press, Chicago, Illinois, 1976.

142 Naimark, Norman M., *Terrorists and Social Democrats: The Russian Revolutionary Movement under Alexander III*, Harvard University Press, Cambridge, Massachusetts, 1983.

143 Offord, Derek, *The Russian Revolutionary Movement in the 1880s*, Cambridge University Press, 1986.

144 Perrie, Maureen, *The Agrarian Policy of the Russian Socialist-Revolutionary Party from Its Origins through the Revolution of 1905–1907*, Cambridge University Press, 1976.

145 Pipes, Richard, *Social Democracy and the St Petersburg Labor Movement, 1885–1897*, Harvard University Press, Cambridge, Massachusetts, 1963; a controversial work which Soviet scholars made a lengthy attempt to rebut.

146 Schapiro, Leonard, *The Communist Party of the Soviet Union*, Eyre and Spottiswoode, 1960; 2nd revised and enlarged edn in University Paperbacks series, Methuen, 1963.

147 Service, Robert, *Lenin: A Political Life*, vol. i, Macmillan, 1985.

148 Ulam, Adam B., *Lenin and the Bolsheviks: The Intellectual and Political History of the Triumph of Communism in Russia*, Secker and Warburg, 1966.

149 Walicki, A., *The Controversy over Capitalism: Studies in the Social Philosophy of the Russian Populists*, Clarendon Press, Oxford, 1969.

150 Woodcock, George, and Ivan Avakumovic, *The Anarchist Prince: A Biographical Study of Peter Kropotkin*, T. V. Boardman, 1950.

INDEX

Adrian, Patriarch (1636–1700), 8
aesthetics, 22, 33, 45, 56, 58, 61
agitation, 70, 72, 74, 79, 81–2, 96, 99
Agrarian Socialist League, 99
Aksakov, I. S. (1823–86), 25, 46, 48
Aksakov, K. S. (1817–60), 25, 27–8, 34, 46, 48; Doc. 10
Aksakov, S. T. (1791–1859), 27
Akselrod, P. B. (1850–1928), 81, 88
Alexander I (born 1777, ruled 1801–25), 2, 12–15, 17, 19; Doc. 2
Alexander II (born 1818, ruled 1855–81), 2, 28, 44–5, 48, 51, 54, 104
assassination of, 82–5, 89, 92–4; Doc. 21
attempts on life of, 63, 81–2
Alexander III (born 1845, ruled 1881–94), 83, 94, 97
Alexander III, the Great (356–23BC), 31
Alexis (born 1629, ruled 1645–76), 4, 8
anarchism, 5, 71, 87; Doc. 23
anarchists, 41, 69, 71–2, 75, 80, 88, 104
Andreiushkin, P. I. (1865–87), 94
Anna, Empress, (born 1693, ruled 1730–40), 3
Annenkov, P. V. (1812 or 1813–87), 29–32, 47, 51, 54

Antonovich, M. A. (1835–1918), 47
Aptekman, O. V. (1849–1926), 81
Arakcheev, General A. A. (1769–1834), 13
Association of St Petersburg Artisans, 95–6

Bakunin, M. A. (1814–76), 29–30, 34, 37, 54, 64, 69–74, 76, 88, 90, 104; Docs 16, 19
Balakirev, M. A. (1836–1910), 62
Baudelaire, Charles (1821–67), 85
Bazhin, N. F. (1843–1908), 66
Bekariukov, D. D. (1861–1934), 94
Belinsky, V. G. (1811–48), 29–30, 33–7, 39, 41–2, 51, 55–6, 104; Doc. 7
Bell, 46
Benckendorff, Count A. Kh. (1781 or 1783–1844), 20, 23
Berdiaev, N. A. (1874–1948), 100
Berlin, Isaiah, 37
Bervi, V. V. (pseudonym Flerovsky; 1829–1918), 67, 76, 95
Bestuzhev-Riumin, M. P. (1803–26), 17
Black Partition, 81, 88, 95, 99
Blagoev, D. N. (1856–1924), 95
Blagoevtsy: *see* Party of Russian Social Democrats
Blanc, Louis (1811–82), 39, 42, 94

Blanqui, Auguste (1805–81), 74
Blanquism, 74; *see also* Jacobinism
Bogoraz, V. G. (1865–1936), 93
Bolívar, Simón (1783–1830), 14
Bolotnikov, I. I. (?–1608), 5
Bolsheviks, 101
Boniface VIII, Pope (*c*. 1235–
1303), Doc. 6
Borisov, A. I. (1798–1854), 16
Borisov, P. I. (1800–1854), 16
Borodin, A. P. (1833–87), 62
Botkin, V. P. (1811–69), 29–32,
34–5, 39, 47, 51, 54
bourgeoisie, 6, 39, 47, 49, 52, 70,
73, 76, 89–91, 100; Docs 20, 22
Breshko-Breshkovskaia, E. K.
(1844–1934), 99
Brusnev, M. I. (1864–1937), 96
Büchner, Ludwig, (1824–99), 58
Buckle, Henry Thomas (1821–62),
50
Buddhism, 85
Bulavin, K. A. (*c*. 1660–1708), 5
Bulgakov, S. N. (1871–1944), 100
Buturlin, General D. P. (1790–
1849), 42

Cabet, Etienne (1788–1856), 42
capitalism, 39–40, 42, 49, 57, 66,
70, 73, 78, 89–92, 95, 100;
Docs 22, 24; *see also*
bourgeoisie, industry,
proletariat, workers
Carbonari, 15
Carr, E. H., 40
Catherine II (Catherine the Great;
born 1729, ruled 1762–96), 3,
9–10, 12, 14, 19, 27, 44
Catholic Church, 7, 24, 28; *see*
also Catholicism
Catholicism, 28, 44; Doc. 11; *see*
also Catholic Church
Cato, Marcus Porcius (234–
149BC), 83
censorship, 2, 13, 20, 22, 42, 50;
Doc. 7

Chaadaev, P. Ia. (1794–1856), 11,
23–5, 38; Doc. 5
Chaikovsky, N. V. (1850–1926),
75; *see also* Chaikovtsy
Chaikovtsy, 75–6, 79, 88
Charlemagne (*c*. 742–814), 31
Charles X (1757–1836; King of
France 1824–30), 57; Doc. 12
Chekhov, A. P. (1860–1904), 85,
98, 126
Chernov, V. M. (1873–1952), 99
Chernyshevsky, N. G. (1828–89),
11, 30, 41, 46–7, 51, 54–63, 66,
68, 75–6, 95, 100, 104; Docs
12, 13
Chicherin, B. N. (1828–1904), 31,
53–4, 104
clergy, 47–8, 77, 102
Committee of the People's
Revenge, 64
conservative thought, 12–14, 25–
30, 34, 46, 48–50, 103–4
Considérant, Victor-Prosper
(1808–93), 42
Constant, Benjamin (1767–1830),
14
Constantine, Grand Duke (1779–
1831), 15, 17
Contemporary, 39, 46, 54, 57, 59,
63, 66
Cossacks, 5
coup d'état, 74, 81, 83, 93; Doc.
20
Crimean War, 41, 44–8, 50, 52–5,
57, 61, 63, 66, 86, 102; Doc. 14
Cui, Ts. A. (1835–1918), 62
Custine, Astolphe, Marquis de
(1790–1857), 25
Czartoryski, Prince A. J. (1770–
1861), 12

Danielson, N. F. (pseudonym
Nikolai -on; 1844–1918), 92
Danilevsky, N. Ia. (1822–85), 41
Dargomyzhsky, A. S. (1813–69),
62

Darwin, Charles, (1809–82), 88
Day, 45
Decembrist Revolt, 13–20, 23, 42;
    see also Decembrists
Decembrists, 2, 11, 13–20, 37, 72,
    103; Docs 2–4; *see also*
    Decembrist Revolt
Deed, 46
Deich, L. G. (1855–1941), 78, 81,
    88, 91
Derzhavin, G. R. (1743–1816), 9,
    12
Dobroliubov, N. A. (1836–61), 30,
    47, 54, 57, 59–61, 104; Doc. 14
Dostoevsky, F. M. (1821–81), 11,
    21, 41, 45–6, 48–50, 65, 85,
    104, 126
Druzhinin, A. V. (1824–64), 46–7,
    51, 54

Eliseev, G. Z. (1821–91), 47
Emancipation of Labour Group,
    88–91, 95
emancipation of serfs, 44–5, 48,
    50–54, 57–8, 60, 62–3, 73, 98;
    Doc. 15; *see also* serfdom
Engels, Friedrich (1820–95), 67,
    71, 73, 83, 89–90, 94; Doc. 22
Epoch, 45

Fedoseev, N. E. (1871–98), 96
Fet, A. A. (1820–92), 60
Feuerbach, Ludwig (1804–72), 38
Fichte, Johann Gottlieb (1762–
    1814), 34
Figner, V. N. (1852–1942), 81,
    93
Flaubert, Gustave (1821–80), 85
Fokin, M. D., 94
Fonvizin, D. I. (1744 or 1745–92),
    9, 12
Forward!, 69–70; Doc. 18
Fourier, Charles (1772–1837), 42,
    69
Freemasonry, 14–16
French Revolution, 30, 32, 50

Gandhi, Mahatma (1869–1948), 88
Generalov, V. D. (1867–87), 94
Gershuni, G. A. (1870–1908), 99
Glinka, M. I. (1804–57), 62
Glinka, S. N. (1775 or 1776–
    1847), 13
Goethe, Johann Wolfgang von
    (1749–1832), 34, 51
Gogol, N. V. (1809–52), 20–22,
    34, 36, 56, 126; Doc. 7
going to the people, 76–7, 98, 103;
    Doc. 19
Goldenberg, G. D. (1855–80), 80
Golitsyn, Prince A. N. (1773–
    1844), 14
Goncharov, I. A. (1812–91), 21,
    45, 60, 126; Doc. 14
Granovsky, T. N. (1813–55), 29–
    31, 38–9, 53, 104; Doc. 6
Grigorev, A. A. (1822–64), 46,
    48–50

Haxthausen, Baron Auguste von
    (1792–1866), 27; Doc. 8
Hegel, Georg Wilhelm Friedrich
    (1770–1831), 34–5, 37–8, 56
Hell (revolutionary cell), 63
Herder, Johann Gottfried von
    (1744–1803), 25
Herwegh, Georg (1817–75), 40
Herzen, A. I. (Gertsen; 1812–70),
    29–30, 37–40, 42, 46, 51, 53–4,
    57, 63, 67, 71, 76, 88, 90, 104;
    Docs 9, 15
Hobbes, Thomas (1588–1679), 74
Holy Alliance, 13–14
Homer, 51

Iakubovich, P. F. (1860–1911), 93
Iakushkin, I. D. (1793–1857), 15
Ignatov, V. N. (d. 1885), 88
industry, 6, 8, 49, 89–90; Doc. 24;
    see also bourgeoisie, capitalism,
    proletariat, workers
intelligentsia, 9–11, 21, 27, 33, 36,
    39, 41–2, 45–7, 51, 53–4, 57,

62, 65–6, 68, 70–72, 74, 78, 83, 85, 90–91, 94, 96–100, 102–5; Docs 7, 17, 19
International Working Men's Association (First International), 71
Ishutin, N. A. (1840–79), 63, 74
Iuzhakov, S. N. (1849–1910), 92
Ivan IV (Ivan the Terrible; born 1530, ruled 1533–84), 1–3, 31
Ivanov, I. I. (d. 1869), 64

Jacobinism, 74, 88–9, 93; Doc. 20; *see also* Jacobins
Jacobins, 20; Doc. 15; *see also* Jacobinism
Joinville, Jean de (*c.* 1224–1317), Doc. 6

Kablits, I. I. (pseudonym Iuzov; 1848–93), 92
Kakhovsky, P. G. (1797–1826), 17
Kantemir, A. D. (1708–44), 9
Karakozov, D. V. (1840–66), 63
Karamzin, N. M. (1766–1826), 13
Kavelin, K. D. (1818–85), 29–31, 49, 51–4, 104
Khomiakov, A. S. (1804–60), 25–6, 28, 46, 48; Doc. 11
Khudiakov, I. A. (1842–76), 63
Kireevsky, I. V. (1806–56), 25–6, 48
Kireevsky, P. V. (1808–56), 25–6, 48
Kniazhnin, Ia. B. (1742–91), 12
Kochubei, Count V. P. (1768–1834), 12
Kosheliov, A. I. (1806–83), 48
Kovalsky, I. M. (1850–78), 80
Kramskoi, I. N. (1837–87), 61
Krasin, L. B. (1870–1926), 96
Kravchinsky, S. M. (pseudonym S.Stepniak; 1851–95), 80
Kremer, A. (1865–1935), 100
Kropotkin, Prince D. N. (1836–79), 80

Kropotkin, Prince P. A. (1842–1921), 69, 75, 80, 88, 104
Kushchevsky, I. A. (1847–76), 66
Kuskova, E. D. (1869–1958), 100

La Harpe, Fréderic-César de (1754–1838), 12
Land and Liberty (1861–2), 63
Land and Liberty (1876–9), 78–83, 101
Lassalle, Ferdinand (1825–64), 94–5
Lavrov, P. L. (pseudonym Mirtov; 1823–1900), 10, 68–73, 76, 88, 95; Docs 17, 18
Left Hegelians: *see* Young Hegelians
legal Marxism, 100
legal Populists, 98
Lenin: *see* V. I. Ulianov
Lermontov, M. Iu. (1814–41), 11, 21, 35
Leroux, Pierre (1797–1871), 39, 42
Levitov, A. I. (1835–77), 61
liberalism, 6, 29–32, 46, 50–54, 57–8, 98; Doc. 12; *see also* liberals
liberals, 17, 29–33, 38–9, 49–54, 56–8, 97–8, 100, 104; Docs 6, 12; *see also* liberalism
Liberation, 98
Library for Reading, 46, 51
literary criticism, 33–6, 49, 51, 56, 59–61; Doc. 14
Liublinsky, Iu. K. (1798–1873), 16
Lomonosov, M. V. (1711–65), 9
Lopatin, G. A. (1845–1918), 69, 93–4
Louis IX of France (born 1214, ruled 1226–70), Doc. 6
Louis XVIII of France (born 1755, ruled 1814–24), 57; Doc. 12

Mably, Gabriel Bonnot de (1709–85), Doc. 1

Magnitsky, M. L. (1778–1855), 13
Maikov, V. N. (1823–47), 41
Maksimov, S. V. (1831–1901), 66
Malia, Martin, 39
Martov: see Iu. O. Tsederbaum
Marx, Karl (1818–83), 32, 70–71, 73, 89–90, 94–6; Doc. 22; see also Marxism
Marxism, 42, 88–91, 95, 99–100, 105; Docs 22, 24; see also Marx
Mensheviks, 101
Menzel, Wolfgang (1798–1873), 34
Miasoedov, G. G. (1834–1911), 61
Michael, Grand Duke (1798–1848), 15, 17
Michelet, Jules (1798–1874), Doc. 9
Mikhailov, A. D. (1855–84), 78, 81
Mikhailov, M. L. (also M. I.; 1826–65), 62
Mikhailovsky, N. K. (1842–1904), 66, 68, 73, 83, 95, 99
Miliutin, N. A. (1818–72), 51
Miloradovich, Count General M. A. (1771–1825), 17
mir: see peasant commune
Mirsky, D. S., 21
Moleschott, Jacob (1822–93), 58
Mordovtsev, D. L. (1830–1905), 66
Morozov, N. A. (1854–1946), 80–81
Moscow Observer, 34
Muraviov, A. N. (1792–1863), 15
Muraviov, N. M. (1796–1843), 15–19; Doc. 3
Muraviov-Apostol, M. I. (1793–1886), 15
Muraviov-Apostol, S. I. (1796–1826), 15, 17
Muscovite, 25, 45
music, 61–2
Musorgsky, M. P. (1839–81), 62

Napoleon Bonaparte (1769–1821), 13, 15, 44; Doc. 2
Napoleonic Wars, 13–15, 102, 104
narodnost', 25, 34
Natanson, M. A. (1850–1919), 75, 99
native-soil conservatism, 45–6, 48–50, 104
Natural School, 36, 41
Nechaev, S. G. (1847–82), 64–5, 74–5; Docs 16, 19
Nechaevtsy, 64–5
Nekrasov, N. A. (1821–77), 21, 29–30, 46, 66, 85
Nicholas I (born 1796, ruled 1825–55), 2, 15, 17, 19–23, 33, 42–6, 54
Nicholas II (1868–1918, ruled 1894–1917), 97
nihilism, 46, 50, 61, 104
nihilists, 47, 61
Nikon, Patriarch (1605–81), 5
nobility, 2–4, 8–9, 12–15, 19, 25, 32, 45, 47, 51–2, 60–61, 102–3; Doc. 2
Northern Society (of Decembrists), 16–17
Northern Union: see Union of Socialist Revolutionaries
Notes of the Fatherland, 34, 41, 46, 66
Novosiltsev, Count N. N. (1761–1836), 12

Obolensky, Prince E. P. (1796–1865), 16
Oboleshev, A. D. (1854–81), 78
obshchina: see peasant commune
Official Nationality, 20, 23
Ogariov, N. P. (1813–77), 37–8, 46, 64
Old Believers: see sectarians
Omulevsky (pseudonym of I. V. Fiodorov; 1836 or 1837–83), 66

Order of Russian Knights, 15
Organization (revolutionary group), 63
Orlov, General M. F. (1788–1842), 15
Orthodox Church, 7–8, 27–8, 77; *see also* Orthodoxy
Orthodoxy, 20, 24, 27–8, 44, 48, 87; Docs 7, 11; *see also* Orthodox Church
Orzhikh, B. D. (1864–after 1934), 93
Oshanina, M. N. (1853–98), 93
Osinsky, V. A. (1852–79), 80
Osipanov, V. S. (1861–87), 94
Ostrovsky, A. N. (1823–86), 45, 126
Owen, Robert (1771–1858), 58, 69

painting, 61–2
Panaev, I. I. (1812–62), 46
Pan-Russian Social-Revolutionary Organization, 79
Paris Commune, 76
Party of Russian Social Democrats, 95
Party of Socialist Revolutionaries, 99
Paul, Emperor (born 1754, ruled 1796–1801), 4, 12–13
peasant commune, 27, 39–40, 42, 48, 57, 66–7, 69–70, 89–91, 95, 104–5; Docs 8, 9, 11, 19, 22, 24
peasant rebellion, 5, 19, 56, 63, 66, 72, 76, 78, 88; Doc. 19
peasantry, 4–5, 19, 27, 38, 40, 47, 49, 52, 54, 56, 60–62, 66–7, 69, 72–4, 76–81, 83, 87, 89–92, 94–5, 98–100, 102; Docs 9, 19, 22, 24; *see also* Russian people
People's Right, 99
People's Will, 11, 81–4, 88, 90–96, 99, 101; Doc. 21
peredvizhniki, 62
Perov, V. G. (1833–82), 61

Perovskaia, S. L. (1853–81), 81–2
Pestel, P. I. (1793–1826), 15–19, 72; Doc. 4
Peter the Great (Peter I; born 1672, sole ruler 1696–1725), 1–4, 7–10, 13, 26, 29, 31, 36
Peter III (born 1728, ruled 1761–62), 3
Petrashevsky, M. V. (1821–66), 41–2
Petrashevtsy, 41–2, 90
Petrunkevich, I. I. (1843–1928), 98
Pisarev, D. I. (1840–68), 30, 59–61, 104
Pisemsky, A. F. (1820–81), 45
Plekhanov, G. V. (1856–1918), 79, 81, 88–91, 99, 105; Doc. 24
Pleshcheev, A. N. (1825–93), 41
Pobedonostsev, K. P. (1827–1907), 97
pogroms, 93
Pole Star, 46
Polish Revolt (of 1863), 53–4, 63
Pomialovsky, N. G. (1835–63), 48
Popko, G. A. (1852–85), 80
Populism, 67, 89, 91, 95, 97–9; *see also* Populists
Populists, 10, 37, 49, 88–92, 95, 98–100; *see also* Populism
Prokopovich, S. N. (1871–1957), 100
proletariat, 27, 57, 61, 71, 79, 89–90, 92, 105; Doc. 8; *see also* workers
propaganda, 70, 72, 74–5, 79–80, 90, 93–5
Proudhon, Pierre-Joseph (1809–65), 39, 42, 70
Pugachov, E. I. (*c.* 1742–75), 5, 72; Doc. 19
Pushkin, A. S. (1799–1837), 12, 19, 21, 24, 34–5, 49, 51, 56, 126; Doc. 14
Putiatin, Count Admiral E. V. (1804–83), 63

Radishchev, A. N. (1749–1802), 10, 12, 67, 69; Doc. 1

rational egoism, 58–60

Razin, S. T. (c. 1630–1671), 5, 72; Doc. 19

raznochintsy, 47–8, 60, 103

Renaissance, 7

Repin, I. E. (1844–1930), 62

Reshetnikov, F. M. (1841–71), 61

Riego y Núñez, Rafael de (1785–1823), 14

Rimsky-Korsakov, N. A. (1844–1908), 62

Robespierre, Maximilien F. M. I. (1758–94), 74

RSDLP (Russian Social-Democratic Labour Party), 100–101

Runich, D. P. (1778–1860), 13

Russian Herald, 46

Russian people, 24, 26–9, 40, 50, 60, 67, 72, 78, 104; Docs 2–4, 7, 10; *see also* peasantry

Russian Wealth, 98

Russian Word, 46

Russo-Turkish War (of 1877–78), 80

Ryleev, K. F. (1795–1826), 16–17

Saint-Simon, Henri de (1760–1825), 37, 39, 42

Saltykov, M. E. (pseudonym Shchedrin; 1826–89), 21, 29, 41, 45, 66

Samarin, Iu. F. (1819–76), 25, 31, 46, 48

Sand, George (pseudonym of Lucie Dudevant, *née* Dupin), 35

Schapiro, Leonard, 1

Schelling, Friedrich (1775–1854), 34, 37

schism, 5

science, 9, 22, 29, 38, 41, 47, 50, 55–6, 59–61, 68, 70, 73, 76, 103; Doc. 13

sectarians, 5, 20, 66, 78, 99

Serafim, Metropolitan (1763–1843), 17

serfdom, 3–6, 10, 12, 15–16, 18, 25, 32–3, 44, 48, 50, 52–3; Doc. 7

Serno-Solovevich, N. A. (1834–66), 63

Shakespeare, William (1564–1616), 51, 61

Shelgunov, N. V. (1824–91), 62

Shevyriov, P. Ia. (1863–87), 94

Shipov, D. N. (1851–1920), 98

Shirinsky-Shikhmatov, Prince P.A. (1790–1853), 42

Shishkov, Admiral A. S. (1754–1841), 13, 20, 25

Siniavsky, A. D. (1925–97), 10

Slavophiles, 25–9, 31, 36, 38, 40–41, 46, 48, 104; Docs 5, 10, 11; *see also* Slavophilism

Slavophilism, 25–31, 45, 48; Docs 5, 10, 11; *see also* Slavophiles

Sleptsov, V. A. (1836–78), 61

small deeds, 85, 98

Social Democracy, 91–2, 95, 97, 100–101

Society of the United Slavs, 16

Society of Translators and Publishers, 94

Sokolov, N. V. (1835–89), 66

Soloviov, A. K. (1846–79), 81

Solzhenitsyn, A. I. (1918–), 88

Southern Party of Socialist Revolutionaries, 99

Southern Society (of Decembrists), 16–17

Speransky, M. M. (1772–1839), 13

Speshnev, N. A. (1821–82), 41

Stasov, V. V. (1824–1906), 62

Stefanovich, Ia. V. (1853–1915), 78, 81

Stirner, Max (pseudonym of Johann Kaspar Schmidt; 1806–56), 41

Strakhov, N. N. (1828–96), 46, 48

Stroganov, Count P. A. (1772–1817), 12

Struve, P. B. (1870–1944), 98, 100
Sturdza, A. S. (1791–1854), 14, 25
Sumarokov, A. P. (1717–77), 9, 12
superfluous man, 22, 24, 38, 60; Doc. 14
Surikov, V. I. (1848–1916), 62

Takhtariov, K. M. (1871–1925), 100
Tamburlaine (1336–1405), 31
Tatar yoke, 1, 7, 26
Telescope, 23, 34
terrorism, 11, 80–84, 91, 93, 95, 99, 103
Third Department, 20; Doc. 16
Third Section: *see* Third Department
Tikhomirov, L. A. (1852–1923), 80–81, 93
Time, 45
Tkachov, P. N. (1844–85), 72–5, 77, 83, 88, 104; Doc. 20
Tochissky, P. V. (1864–1918), 95–6
Tocsin, 73; Doc. 20
Tolstoy, L. N. (1828–1910), 21, 45, 67, 69, 71, 85–8, 104, 126; Doc. 23
Tolstoyism, 85, 87
Tönnies, Ferdinand Julius (1855–1936), 26
Trepov, General F. F. (1812–89), 80
trial of the 50, 79
trial of the 193, 77, 79
Trubetskoi, Prince S. P. (1790–1860), 15–17
Tsederbaum, Iu. O. (i.e. Martov; 1873–1923), 99–100
Tugan-Baranovsky, M. I. (1865–1919), 100
Tugendbund, 14, 16
Turgenev, I. S. (1818–83), 5, 11, 21, 29–30, 32, 42, 45–7, 51–2, 54, 56, 60–61, 85, 126

Turgot, Anne-Robert-Jacques (1727–81), 58

Ulianov, A. I. (1866–87), 94, 96–7
Ulianov, V. I. (i.e. Lenin; 1870–1924), 55, 73, 96–7, 99–100, 104
Union of Liberation, 98
Union of Salvation, 15–16
Union of Socialist Revolutionaries, 99
Union of Struggle for the Liberation of the Working Class, 100
Union of Welfare, 16
Uspensky, N. V. (1837–89), 47, 56, 61
Uvarov, Count S. S. (1786–1855), 20, 42

Varangians, 29, 49
Vereshchagin, V. V. (1842–1904), 62
Vischer, Friedrich Theodor von (1807–87), 56
Vladimir (born *c*. 956, Grand Prince of Kiev *c*. 980–1015), 7
Vogt, Karl (1817–95), 58
Voices from Russia, 51, 54
Vorontsov, V. P. (1847–1918), 92

Walicki, Andrzej, 26
Wanderers: *see peredvizhniki*
Westernism, 29–32; *see also* Westernizers
Westernizers, 29–41, 46–7, 56, 104; Docs 5, 6; *see also* Westernism
Witte, Count S. Iu. (1849–1915), 97
workers, 6, 67, 75–7, 79, 82, 89–90, 92–6, 99–100; Doc. 24; *see also* proletariat
Workers' Cause, 100
Workers' Thought, 100

Young Hegelians, 37–8, 70
Ypsilantis, Alexander (1792–1828), 15

Zaichnevsky, P. G. (1842–96), 63; Doc. 15

Zasulich, V. I. (1849–1919), 80–81, 88
zemstva, 97–8, 104
Zheliabov, A. I. (1851–81), 81–2
Zlatovratsky, N. N. (1845–1911), 92